CONTENTS

D1221680

**For my parents, Edith and Heinz,
and my sisters, Heike and Doris**

Since the completion of this book of essays, we heard
the very sad news of Detlef Mertins' terribly premature
death on 14 January 2011. Detlef was a brilliant scholar
and wonderful person, and I hope that this collection
offers some kind of register of the enduring qualities
of his architectural voice.
— Brett Steele

Detlef Mertins (1954–2011)

INTRODUCTION

BY DETLEF MERTINS

Modernity, it may be worth remembering, has a history, or, as the literary critic Marshall Berman put it, the *experience* of modernity has a history – an experience that is expressed, preserved and made accessible through literature and other forms of culture. Over five hundred or so years, the experience of modernity has undergone major transformations in relation to the changing scale, scope and location of modernisation, successive paradigms in science, technology and thought, and the structure of power and organisation of social relations. In his book, *All That is Solid Melts into Air* (1982), Berman observed that from the beginning of the sixteenth century up to the end of the eighteenth century, people in Europe began to experience the displacements and conflicts of modern life but had no vocabulary to express them or community within which hopes and trials could be shared. It was through the great revolutionary wave of the 1790s that the modern public erupted into life, ushering in the feeling of living in a revolutionary age, one in which everything was beginning again. Yet people continued to remember how things used to be, leading to a sense of living in two worlds at once. This tense inner dichotomy was described by Rousseau as a whirlwind of dread and wonder, clash and flux.

The nineteenth century, in turn, produced a new landscape of conflicts and dialectics, of steam engines, railways, industrial zones, spectacular wealth, great cities and bourgeois suburbs and, at the same time, dreadful poverty, degraded living and working conditions, waste, disease and devastation. Remarkably, people managed to make themselves at home. As much a student of words as of politics, Berman noted that even political critics such as Marx needed verbal images to conquer modernity – intense images of personal and social abysses, earthquakes and volcanic eruptions, images such as Berman's title, 'all that is solid melts into air'.[1]

During its third phase, in the twentieth century, modernity lost steam, according to Berman; for as modernisation expanded to encompass the entire world, the modern public fragmented into a multitude of incommensurable private languages. Furthermore, Berman lamented that twentieth-century thinkers about modernity suffered 'a radical flattening of perspective and shrinkage of imaginative range'.[2] The dialectical energies of modernity in the nineteenth century were eclipsed in the early twentieth century by claims that a new unity had been achieved under the rubric of 'modernism'. Critics lurched toward rigid polarities (either/or instead of both/and) and flat totalisations. Open conceptions of modern life were supplanted by closed ones, with limited capacity for participation or change. Writing in the early 1980s, after the disillusionment of student protests in 68, Berman argued that it was time to renew the dynamic and dialectical modernism of the nineteenth century, to illuminate once again the contradictory forces at play and restore the openness and expansiveness that had been lost.

While one may take issue with various aspects of Berman's periodisation and characterisations – for instance, his neglect of so many other avant-garde artists and writers who kept dialectical, corrosive and negative thought alive in the twentieth century – it is remarkable how frequently the general outline of such a history has been reiterated not only in literary criticism but in most other fields of study. Yet Berman is unique, I believe, for having identified so sharply the reduction in scope and dynamics in so much of modernism in the twentieth century. In my own fields, architecture and urbanism, the rhetoric of struggles and battles admittedly continued but was accompanied by an unprecedented conviction in a new model. Claims to a new unity of cultural expression abound in early to mid-twentieth-century architectural discourse, where the authority of Otto Wagner (*Moderne Architektur*, 1900), for instance, was to have resolved the deep longing within the field for an all-embracing new style; where Le Corbusier achieved pre-eminence over all other architects of the twentieth century through his masterful gamesmanship as well as the play of volumes in light; and where Henry-Russell Hitchcock and Philip C Johnson's *International Style* exhibition at the newly minted Museum of Modern Art in New York (1932) did more to codify modern architecture than any other thing, apart from Sigfried Giedion's more belaboured and less understood history of some years later, *Space, Time, and Architecture* (1941).

Modernity designates what is distinct about a specific moment in time whose duration, however, may vary from a sunset to a century. *Modernisation*, on the other hand, refers to transformations of materialist civilisation – improvements in plumbing, material efficiencies, rationalisation of transportation, accounting and window schedules. In contrast to both, *modernism* may be thought of as the cultural response to modernity and modernisation, a response that aspires to the status of a new norm. As the philosopher Jürgen Habermas once observed, modernity cannot follow models from another epoch; 'it has to create its normativity out of itself'.[3]

If, as Mies van der Rohe put it, the years after 1900 were still ones of uncertainty, it was precisely Mies's generation, the generation of the 1880s – Le Corbusier, Walter Gropius, Giedion – who would succeed in claiming the mantle of the truly modern. Their success owed much, as Beatriz Colomina has shown, to their deft use of the new mass media. More than any media of the past, print, photography and film in the early twentieth century had the capacity to create a unified mass audience, susceptible to receiving a strong unified message.

Thirty or forty years ago, architectural history was dominated by a few major books on modern architecture that provided narratives of epochal identity along with introductions to major figures, movements and themes. Nikolaus Pevsner's *Pioneers of Modern Design* (1936) was still often read, although it had long been displaced by Giedion's weightier and more dramatic *Space, Time, and Architecture*. Where Pevsner considered the Bauhaus under Walter Gropius as exemplary of modernism and rooted it in the arts and crafts movement in England, Giedion defined it in terms of a new space concept – space–time – aligned with modern science and modern art and realised through new technology. Giedion recognised its seed in the spatial complexities of the baroque, but considered it finally fulfilled only in the work of his friend, Le Corbusier. A student of both Pevsner and Giedion, Reyner Banham took issue with machine symbolism and focused his account in *Theory and Design in the First Machine Age* (1960) on rationalism, futurism and the American inventor, R Buckminster Fuller. That same year, Leonardo Benevelo produced his two-volume *Modern Architecture* (1960), which placed even greater emphasis than Giedion had on the industrial vernacular and modern town planning, subsuming leading figures and high design within broader societal and environmental transformations. Although these books differed significantly in what they took to be the origins of modernism, its defining traits and even key figures, they could still be seen as complementary. Their differences left intact the conviction that modern architecture was a single unified historical phenomenon. Having begun by challenging pre-existing codes, it succumbed to its own codification.

Only gradually did the monolithic construct of modern architecture begin to crack and the modern movement's claims come to appear more a desire than a reality. As a younger generation of modern architects challenged the leadership of the masters and the dominant formulas of CIAM (Team X, Ernesto Rogers, Philip Johnson), so too a younger generation of historians began to offer alternative histories of greater complexity and irresolution. Joseph Rykwert (*The First Moderns*, 1980), Manfredo Tafuri (*The Sphere and the Labyrinth*, 1980) and

Anthony Vidler (*The Writing of the Walls: Architectural Theory of the Late Enlightenment*, 1987) each staked claims to the origin of modernism in a different time, place and temperament (seventeenth or eighteenth century; functionalist, dialectical or reformist). For them, it was a contest in which the definition, and hence future, of modernism was always at stake. During these times, the pantheon of heroes was also expanded to include minor figures who had not fitted into previous master narratives (Alvar Aalto, Guiseppi Terragni, Erich Mendelsohn). In this effort, Kenneth Frampton's *Modern Architecture: A Critical History* (1981) provided a bountiful resource.

The research that Tafuri launched at this time was especially important for breaking up the master narrative by looking for contradictions and contestations that would parallel in architecture the dialectical transformations and political struggles of industrial capitalism. To understand the motive forces of modern architecture in capitalist America and bourgeois Europe, Tafuri applied conceptual tools from the 'critical theory' of the Frankfurt School (Adorno, Horkheimer, Benjamin), which had pioneered cultural criticism based on Marxist analysis. He discerned the dialectics of Enlightenment at work in architecture and urbanism just as Adorno and Horkheimer had done more broadly within American culture; they had shown that the rise of rationality did not banish myth but rather repressed and channelled it into new myths that obscured the operations of power. In *Architecture and Utopia: Design and Capitalist Development* (1973), *Modern Architecture* (1979, with Francesco Dal Co) and *Sphere and Labyrinth* (1980), Tafuri gave priority to the left wing of European functionalism – Mart Stam, Hannes Meyer and Ernst May – and to liberal reform movements in America and constructivism in Russia.

During the late 1980s and early 1990s yet another generation of historians shifted focus once more, this time to the writing of history itself and the construction of architectural discourse in the broadest sense. This foregrounded the inevitable biases of historical studies and the propensity of modernist histories to present narratives of internally coherent linear development when the reality was jagged, messy and included an ever-proliferating cast of figures and an ever-expanding field of contestations. Colomina demonstrated how the discourse of modern architecture – and modern architecture itself – was shaped by the new media of photography, film and print in the 1920s and by the proliferation of small magazines and journals through which careers could be made without actually building much. Hélène Lipstadt showed the formative role of journals and competitions already in the nineteenth century, while Joan Ockman, Gwendolyn Wright, Terence Riley and others studied the media in the recent past and extended the research into institutions of discourse-formation such as schools, museums and galleries. Werner Oechslin and his colleagues at the GTA reconstructed the self-constructions of CIAM, Giedion and Le Corbusier, while Mark Wigley explored the blind spots routinely left out of such pictures yet crucial to their very existence, evidence 'nestled between the lines of the all too familiar literature, hidden only because it is so close to our eyes'.[4]

Histories began to appear of women who had first been written out of the master narratives (Eileen Gray, Charlotte Perriand, Lilly Reich) and of non-Western modernisms and their engagement with the dynamics and tensions of modernisation as it spread throughout the world. All this demonstrated that the production of architecture, like the production of philosophy, depends on its disciplinary apparatus, textuality or matrix. Every new work is constituted by this matrix and is, in turn, constitutive of it. This reciprocity is key to the performative character of the matrix, which, in turn, gives it the capacity to change. Language, for instance, does not exist *as such* but only through its use, which can be inflected and changed. If modernism was not monolithic after all and did not happen by itself, if neither history nor capitalism are forces of nature but rather social constructions, then they could potentially have taken different courses and produced different results. The fact that the history of modern architecture was full of struggles both within generations and between them, underscores this possibility. Even if what architects and theorists fought about was nothing more than whose version would triumph, modernism gains an unexpected uncertainty while a sphere of action opens up for its protagonists.

Yet, is 'anything goes' good enough in this plural state? Is it sufficient simply to enjoy the proliferation of modern*isms*? With his *Five Faces of Modernity* (1977–87), the literary critic Matei Calinescu provided helpful distinctions between modernism, avant-garde, decadence, kitsch and post-modernism as cultural positions, while Peter Bürger, in *Theory of the Avant-Garde* (1974–84), sharpened what was at stake in the debates over the autonomy of art and its engagement with life, working through the traumas of historical experience. Perhaps modernism can acquire a different kind of unity if we take it to be not an entity or proposition at all, but rather a question with many possible answers, some of which are better than others. If as Berman suggested, modernism is a cultural response to the conditions of modernisation, the question might simply be how should cultural production respond to these conditions? Should it celebrate, repress or ameliorate the traumas of industrialisation? How should it engage with the exhilaration and risks of new technologies? Formulated this way, modernism is no longer a thing but a relationship and the terms for its appraisal need to be revised accordingly. For instance, is the relationship enabling or inspiring? How adequate is a work – in material, formal, representational or experiential terms – to the problematics of modernity that it addresses, be it intentionally or not? In this, history may assume a new urgency as a necessary context or epistemic frame within or against which to conceive and evaluate work. Perhaps this would overly privilege the history of the recent present, but often what we think are strictly contemporary issues prove to have previous iterations, often many and much earlier.

I began writing as an historian in the late 1980s with

the modest goal of helping to expand the main narrative of modernism to include my hometown, Toronto, where modern architecture only took seed in the 1940s and blossomed in the postwar period. I was part of a collective research group (BAU) and part of a younger generation of architects (actually a second generation) who were inspired by the early local moderns and sought to recognise and protect their work from needless demolition. Around 1990, I shifted my attention to the history of architectural theory interpretations and revelations. I came to focus on things that had been misunderstood or overlooked in the historical record and could, therefore, serve as mediators for new thought and design. The writing of architectural history can close down the past or open it up anew. It can bind historical experience into yet another *ism* – how many moderni*sms* do we already have, how many can we possibly need? – or it can unlock the life and *modernité* that resides even in the modernisms we already have. More often than not, that has been the underlying project of the essays assembled in this volume.

For instance, the history of glass architecture has long been misunderstood, having been affiliated too closely with Bruno Taut and his Crystal Chain Circle in the years 1919–20. As my essays, 'Glass Architecture' and 'The Utopia of Glass' reveal, the enthusiasm for Paul Scheerbart's mock treatise, *Glass Architecture* (1914), as well as his poems and asteroid fantasies, extended widely among the artistic avant-garde, most surprisingly to the dadaists, the constructivist László Moholy-Nagy and the literary critic Walter Benjamin. For Scheerbart, glass architecture designated the complete industrialisation of the environment, through which, he imagined, wonders could be achieved again and again – lighting up the night with electricity or flying around the globe, things that we now take for granted but at the time seemed magical.

Needless to say, the range of interpretations was highly varied and could even be dark, as in Benjamin's essay of 1933 on the impoverishment of experience that would be brought on by such a fully technological environment. For Benjamin, a dystopian glass architecture now provided the only possible model for living through the brutality of fascism, which was just beginning. In my essay on Benjamin and the 'tectonic unconscious', I explore a link between glass architecture and the new optics of photography and film through which a new landscape was seen to open up, charged once more with utopian aspirations but radically circumscribed as something that could only ever be glimpsed and never realised.

The related topic of transparency has likewise been widely misunderstood, dominated in America since the 1950s by Colin Rowe and Robert Slutzky's distinction between 'literal' and 'phenomenal' species. When transparency, translucency and opacity regained their importance in design culture in the late 1980s, architects and theorists were hampered by this distinction but unable simply to jettison it. Not only was there nothing literal about the transparency of Gropius, Moholy-Nagy and the constructivist avant-garde, but the 'phenomenal transparency' that Rowe and Slutzky espoused was impossible to understand and torturous to apply, based as it was on the premise that buildings should conform to a long outdated and erroneous theory of vision as fundamentally two-dimensional. As my essays 'Anything But Literal' and 'Transparency: Autonomy and Relationality' show, this distinction's only real achievement was to divide progressive art and architecture into two opposed camps whose protagonists had, however, never seen themselves as engaged in such a fight and instead shared many of the same goals.

By revivifying Giedion's conception of transparency, I was able to reconstruct a broader and more inclusive field of discourse about the topic among expressionists, purists, elementalists and constructivists, one that was far more nuanced, had a richer history of experimentation and greater potential for practice than Rowe and Slutzky's reductive and restrictive interpretation. For them, transparency relied on an observer stationed on axis with a two-dimensional plane (a painting or the facade of a building), immobile and devoid of thought and action. Yet for Giedion and his constructivist colleagues, it was a function of a four-dimensional spatiality activated by a mobile and participatory subject. Giedion described this as a 'relational' space rather than a space of objects.

Much of my work on Mies has focused on his previously overlooked conception of life, which was fuelled on the one hand by an organicism that was widely shared (but also widely unacknowledged) among his generation, and on the other by his readings in the life sciences and the philosophy of life and its successors – the phenomenology of Max Scheler and Eduard Spranger, the existentialism of Karl Jaspers and the existential theology of Romano Guardi and Jacques Maritain. My essay 'Same Difference' begins by reviewing the familiar critique of Mies's gridded glass boxes as rigid and totalitarian, demanding conformity by their inhabitants to a restrictive way of life envisaged by the architect in advance. This argument repeats Adolf Loos's earlier critique of architecture as a total work of art and yet Mies's spaces are equally renowned for their emptiness and austerity, seen by some as terrifyingly 'unliveable' and by others as exhilarating. While Edith Farnsworth found her glass house more challenging than comforting, Grete and Fritz Tugendhat defended their house in Brno from accusations by critics who had never even visited it, declaring how much they enjoyed the magisterial serenity of the great glass living room in which everything and everybody came into sharper relief. Where Mies shared a commitment to the reform of everyday life, his buildings allowed life to be lived large, even experimentally.

In my essay 'Mies's Event Space', I show that at the New National Gallery in Berlin Mies knew full well that the great glass exhibition hall would be difficult to use for conventional shows of conventional paintings (after all, it was intended for temporary shows and not the historical painting collection, which was displayed well in the galleries below). He said there was perhaps a better way to display art – perhaps to 'do it' – and he would not want to miss that. In the case of both his domestic and institutional buildings, Mies positioned himself at the cutting edge of the new, although he also drew the new back to the past. He once said his work was both progressive and conservative, charging it with unresolved tensions that kept the occupant in a perpetual state of motion and self-formation.

My research on Mies also explored his preoccupation with the sciences, especially biology and including the 'biotechnics' advocated by botanist Raoul H Francé in the early to mid-1920s. Francé was popular among artists and architects of the time, especially those who had been associated more with constructivism and the embrace of new technology than with the idea of designing with nature: El Lissitzky, László Moholy-Nagy, his Bauhaus pupil Siegfried Ebeling, Bauhaus director Hannes Meyer and Erno Kallai, appointed by Meyer to edit the Bauhaus journal. If the link between biologism and constructivism is surprising today, we may do well to remember that Michel Foucault had emphasised the paradigmatic role of biology in the modern period in his *The Order of Things*. It became teasing to explore further the links, similarities and differences between this discourse in the 1920s and the one of recent years. The last 15 years have certainly witnessed a renewed fascination in architecture and design with natural models and principles, be they biological, geological or ecological. Greg Lynn and others who pioneered the use of dynamic computer modelling for architectural form in the mid-1990s recognised its potential to support a generative way of designing that is analogous to the development and growth of cells. While Lynn's forms are now directly biomorphic (biomorphism in the 1930s was partly inspired by Francé), it is salutary to realise that very similar terms were ascribed almost a century ago to forms and technologies that were mechanical.

When asked by Lars Spuybroek to contribute to his book, *NOX: Machining Architecture*, I chose to explore a parallel preoccupation to that of the cell among scientists, artists, architects and engineers: the tiny microscopic sea creatures known as radiolarians, first discovered and promoted as prototypes for design by the German evolutionist Ernst Haeckel around 1900. Spuybroek followed the lead of Frei Otto who, in the 1970s, developed what he called analogical models for self-directed form-finding processes across a large range of natural phenomena. Where mid-century figures such as R Buckminster Fuller celebrated the mathematical regularity and purity of radiolarians, Otto realised this was a mistake, since ever more powerful microscopes revealed irregularities in the creatures' cellular shells. Moreover, regularity was necessary only to the top-down kind of cosmology that Fuller espoused, not the bottom-up logistics of materialists such as Otto and Spuybroek. The entire cosmology of mid-century shell structures – from the most elemental units would arise the most complex structures – could come crashing down and yet the universe would not in fact follow suit.

Many more histories should be written to explore the antecedents of today's ecological and biologistic architectures. They should be inclusive, from the high-tech high-performance structures of Norman Foster, Renzo Piano and Richard Rogers to the morphogenesis of younger designers such as Michael Weinstock, Michael Hensel, Achim Menges, Jenny Sabin, Philip Beesley and many more – if only to remind us that what we take to be authoritative today will be superseded in time, just as the authorities of the past have been. Writing many histories will sponsor the proliferation of new experiments, some of which may lead to true innovation while others may just remain extraordinary events that mark a specific moment and perspective in time.

The essays collected here do not present a single argument, nor do they form a book in the sense that a book is a whole. As a whole, it remains unbound. While I hope the essays share an approach, there is considerable air between and within them. Each of my stories opens up material we thought we knew, and tries to keep it open rather than closing it down once more. Each revises an episode of the history of modern architecture, without however venturing to rewrite that history as such. Each is open and unbounded, expansive, restless and unresolved. Together, they begin to suggest a modernity that takes difference (alterity) to be its core. As the architects of humanity seek to manage and control the world ecosystem ever more – perhaps there is little option left but to attempt that – it becomes crucial to safeguard whatever movement of difference that one can, to keep the system from locking down on itself, by whatever means one has at one's disposal, even in the relatively marginal realm of architectural history.

NOTES

1. Marshall Berman, *All That is Solid Melts into Air: The Experience of Modernity* (New York: Simon and Schuster, 1982).

2. Ibid., 24.

3. Jürgen Habermas, *The Philosophical Discourse of Modernity: Twelve Lectures*, trans. Frederick Lawrence (Cambridge, MA: MIT Press, 1990), 7.

4. Mark Wigley, *White Walls, Designer Dresses: The Fashioning of Modern Architecture* (Cambridge, MA: MIT Press, 1995), xv.

GLASS ARCHITECTURE

Is glass still glass? Notwithstanding the significant changes that have taken place in technology and culture since the early twentieth century, it can be said that glass is *still* glass because it never was *just* glass. Glass architecture was and continues to be both technological *and* cultural, mobilised in the service of aesthetic affects that are sometimes weak and sometimes strong.

The Berlin bohemian, poet and fantasist Paul Scheerbart launched the idea of *Glass Architecture* in his book of that name in 1914 – a mock technical treatise in which he described many kinds of glass, some old as well as new: majolica tiles from 1000 BC and Gothic stained glass, along with wired glass, glass blocks, glass fibres, coloured Tiffany glass and even double glass walls with light and heating in between.[1] However, he also described structures of iron skeletons and reinforced concrete, jointless magnesite floor covering, cladding of enamelled and porcelain panels, ventilators on the outside of windows, heating and cooling appliances and even vacuum cleaners for outside as well as in. In fact, he circumscribed the entire world of modern technology, including electric streetlights, steam and electric trains, and aeroplanes. For Scheerbart and many who followed him, glass architecture had the scope of total reconstruction of the world – 'remaking the crust of the earth' for the pleasure as well as comfort of all people. If Scheerbart's prose was, as Walter Benjamin later observed, dry and technical, the world that he envisioned was full of technical wonders, no longer disenchanted by modernisation but re-enchanted in a new stage of evolution ushered in by the magic of inventors.[2]

Inspired by Scheerbart's science fantasies, the architect Bruno Taut sought his collaboration in his well-known Glass House, a demonstration pavilion for the glass industry at the industrial exhibition of the Deutscher Werkbund in 1914 in Cologne. While he called it the Glass House, its structure was reinforced concrete and none of the glass was, in fact, transparent. Instead he used hollow glass blocks at the base as well as for stairs and floors, coloured glass lenses for the cupola, and brightly coloured mosaics for the walls of the cascade room below, through which visitors descended toward a large kaleidoscope before being released to the outside once more. The cupola had a remarkably fine ribbed structure in a shape reminiscent of organic forms such as acorns or the microscopic sea creatures known as radiolarians, which the biologist Ernst Haeckel discovered in the 1880s and popularised around 1900 in his book *Art Forms of Nature*. For Taut, as for Scheerbart, glass architecture represented a new stage in the development of technology that promised to reintegrate humanity with nature.

Taut's aim was not a naive return to pre-modern craft but a return forward to a new nature, a second and synthetic nature achieved by humanity but in accordance with nature's laws. It is not insignificant that glass, iron and concrete are all synthetic materials not found in nature but fashioned by transforming natural materials. Glass architecture served to designate a world that was a compound – 100 per cent human and 100 per cent natural – the result of natural evolution and technological development rolled into one. In this world, it was understood that technologies were transparent when their technical forms were perfected so as to express their immanent logics – material, mathematical and functional. The geometric perfection of their morphology gave them the character of a crystal, while their capacity to perform functions and do work gave them the character of living organisms.

Finally, for Scheerbart and Taut, glass architecture created a new environment for new kinds of experience; in fact, for a new subjectivity. The Glass House provided an immersive artistic environment – a total work of art integrating glass construction, glass art and mosaics –

which induced an altered state of consciousness or delirium as the subject dissolved empathetically to be at one with the world.

After the First World War, Taut proposed a visionary 'Alpine architecture' that would rehouse the population of

industrial metropolises, such as Berlin, in new garden cities of glass constructions distributed in clusters in the Alps, literally remaking the crust of the earth. Others in Taut's Crystal Chain group offered similar fantasies. The artist Wenzel Hablik, for instance, imagined iron and glass towers growing from the ground like living crystals – remarkably similar to the torqued towers that are springing up all over the world today. Drawing on living creatures and plants instead of crystals, Hermann Finsterlin

Wenzel Hablik, Exhibition Tower, Variation 4A II, 1921

dreamt of glass constructions as amorphous growths that resembled molluscs and snails as well as blown glass.

Inspired by the critic Adolf Behne, who reconceptualised the terms of glass architecture in his *The Return of Art* (*Wiederkehr der Kunst*) of 1919 – characterising glass as cubist and biological – the Hungarian suprematist and self-styled artist-engineer László Moholy-Nagy launched his own multi-year exploration of these themes with a painting of 1921–22 entitled *Glass Architecture*. At that time, he also introduced constructivist pedagogy at the Bauhaus, mining the potentials of new materials, media and technologies. From his transparent paintings to lithographs, photograms, photographs and stage sets, he constructed effects of transparency through overlapping planes and pursued a dynamic and interactive conception of space. He imagined kinetic constructions with which the observer would interact in motion, both physically and perceptually. In 1929, he concluded his book on Bauhaus teaching with a negative photomontage representing a future architecture of glass that the next generation would be the first to experience. That same year, he produced a film, *Light Play*, which simulated the visual effects of a subject floating in a fluid space of light and reflection, moving amongst the high-tech elements of a rotating apparatus called the Light–Space Modulator.

In his writings of the late 1920s Moholy referred explicitly to the theories of biotechnics published by the botanist Raoul H Francé. Francé's writings on science and technology came to the attention of the Berlin art world around 1923 and inspired other artists and architects, including El Lissitzky, Mies van der Rohe, Siegfried Ebeling and Hannes Meyer.[3] By the mid-1920s, what had begun as future visions of glass culture, architecture and urbanism had been inflected towards an explicitly biocentric and biotechnic world-view among figures usually associated with 'international constructivism' and thought to be enamoured of technology. While Scheerbart did not use the term 'biotechnics', it may be apt for any architecture that aspires to the status of a second nature. I have coined the term 'bioconstructivism' in order to foreground not just the biological dimension of this strain of constructivist art and architecture but also the constructive and generative orientation of biological theories that seek to describe how nature builds living creatures and ecologies. Bioconstructivism is not, I hasten to add, a term that was used at the time.

While the larger field of bioconstructivist work is beyond the scope of the present essay, I will focus for a moment on an issue of Kurt Schwitters' journal *Merz* which was guest-edited with El Lissitzky in 1924 and entitled 'Nasci'. *Nasci* is a Latin word with a complex meaning that includes natural growth and approximates the German term *Gestaltung*, which refers to the process of generating form. Lissitzky's text begins by distancing himself from the ideology of the machine, which had become too reductive:

We have had enough of perpetually hearing Machine, Machine, Machine when it comes to modern art-production. The machine is no more than a brush and a very primitive one at that... All tools set forces in motion,

which are directed to the crystallising of amorphous nature – which is the aim of nature itself…. The machine has not separated us from nature; through it we have discovered a new nature never before surmised… Our work is a limb of nature…[4]

Lissitzky went on to explain that art and science had both managed to reduce form to its basic elements, which could then be used to reconstruct entities according to the universal laws of nature. In so doing both had arrived at 'the same formula: every form is the frozen instantaneous picture of a process. Thus a work is a stopping-place on the road of becoming and not the fixed goal.' Lissitzky was interested in works that 'contain a system within them-selves', understanding a system as evolving in the course of a work rather than preceding it. His goal was to design 'the peace of nature, in which enormous tensions hold the heavenly bodies, rotating uniformly, in equal balance'.[5]

Taking a page from Francé's book, *Die Pflanze als Erfinder* (The Plant as Inventor), Lissitzky explained that all of creation was the result of seven technical forms: crystal, sphere, plane, rod, ribbon, screw and cylinder. Everything in the universe – architecture, machine elements, crystals and chemicals, geography and astronomical formations, art and technology – was built up from these fundamental elements. Next to his text, he presented one of his own Proun constructions as demonstrative of these principles and goals.

Turning the pages of the journal, we find a diverse array of further examples of biotechnics in modern art and architecture: a neo-plasticist painting by Piet Mondrian and a collage by Kurt Schwitters; a sculpture by Archipenko and a collage by Hans Arp; Mies van der Rohe's curvilinear glass skyscraper of 1922 juxtaposed with a pavilion by JJP Oud and a human femur bone (redrawn by El Lissitzky after Francé); a lithograph by Fernand Léger and Vladimir Tatlin's design for the *Monument to the Third International* of 1919 (a structure with large volumes that were to rotate within an open steel framework: a cube, a sphere and a cylinder); another collage, this time by Georges Braque, and a dark yet luminous photograph of a crystal.

Looking outside the magazine, yet within Lissitzky's work of the same time, his *Wolkenbügel* project for major intersections in Moscow of 1924–25 provides a further demonstration of Francé's principles and of Lissitzky's idea of architecture participating in a dynamic universe where

El Lissitzky, Der Wolkenbügel (Cloud Stirrup), 1924–25

structures are momentary stopping-places along the way in endless processes of becoming, through which amorphous nature takes form only to dissolve again into formlessness. Lissitzky's well-known 'Self-Portrait' of 1924–25 is indicative of a conception of the new human subject – a kind of cyber-constructor whose vision is enhanced by optical instruments such as microscopes, telescopes and x-rays, and whose physical capacities are augmented by mechanistic extensions of limbs and body actions.

Francé's call for a biotechnic rethinking of architecture and engineering became important for architects as far apart ideologically as Mies van der Rohe and Hannes Meyer. At Columbia University in 1939 Friedrich Kiesler propounded a biotechnic theory that was more fully ecological and evolutionary than the approaches of either Moholy or Lissitzky. Like them, he was interested in formative processes and not just form, in the performance and expansion of the human brain and senses through technology.

I hope that even this brief rereading of history reveals that avant-garde experiments with engineering and new media in the early twentieth century treated glass as much more than 'just glass' and that the glass culture envisioned by expressionists and constructivists sought to reintegrate humanity in nature, enhance life and revitalise experience. As we proceed into the twenty-first century – often characterised as post-industrial and biotechnic, the age of genetic engineering, digital media, nanotechnology and 'cradle to cradle' design – it may be helpful to work through this history more thoroughly as a prehistory of our own aspirations: our desire for ecologically benign technologies that enable buildings to perform increasingly as if they were alive. Earlier generations have left us a rich resource of work and thought that should be mined, corrected and updated.

The fact that much of this history was forgotten in the campaign to forge a unified hegemonic modern movement should be salutary for us, a reminder that we no longer need to do that. Insistence on a universal 'ism' has, thankfully, subsided, at least to a large extent. Instead, experimental schools of architecture are actively renewing the culture of experimentation as a more heterogeneous, inclusive and open-ended alternative to monolithic, exclusive and dogmatic conceptions of architectural practice. A fuller treatment of the history I have offered today would, of course, need to distinguish between the use of science to legitimise the totalising visions of modern architects and its role as a stimulus for experimentations that need not be assimilated to new totalities. It is in this respect that glass is no longer glass, as the commanding signifier of a social utopia. Rather, today's glass architects may be seen to participate in the evolution of the planet through the production of unassimilable diversity, one experiment at a time. Their work is consistent with Darwinian ideas which explain how evolution occurs over many iterations and many generations, its progress depending on the production of diversity, of 'endless forms most beautiful and most wonderful'.[6]

NOTES

1. Paul Scheerbart, *Glasarchitektur* (Berlin: Verlag der Sturm, 1914). English edition, *Glass Architecture*, translated by James Palmes (New York: Praeger, 1972).

2. For Walter Benjamin's reading of Scheerbart see my essay 'The Enticing and Threatening Face of Prehistory: Walter Benjamin and the Utopia of Glass' on pages 88–113 of this volume.

3. Raoul H Francé, 'Die sieben technischen Grundformen der Natur', *Das Kunstblatt* 7:1 (January 1923), 5–11. The article is excerpted from Francé, *Die Pflanze als Erfinder* (Stuttgart: Kosmos, 1920). English translation *Plants as Inventors* (Stuttgart: Jung & Sons, 1923). For Francé's reception in the Berlin art world, see Oliver Botar, *Prolegomena to the Study of Biomorphic Modernism: Biocentrism, László Moholy-Nagy's 'New Vision', and Ernó Kállai's Bioromantik*, PhD thesis, University of Toronto, 1998.

4. El Lissitzky, 'Nasci', *Merz* 8–9 (April–June 1924).

5. El Lissitzky, 'Nasci'.

6. In concluding *On the Origin of Species* (first published in 1859), Darwin claimed a certain grandeur for his new view that the manifold powers of life had been 'originally breathed into a few forms or into one; and that… from so simple a beginning endless forms most beautiful and most wonderful have been, and are being, evolved'. See Charles Darwin, *On the Origin of Species* (Cambridge, MA & London: Harvard University Press, 1964), 490.

ANYTHING BUT LITERAL:
SIGFRIED GIEDION AND THE RECEPTION
OF CUBISM IN GERMANY

For the past 30 years, the significance of cubism for modern architecture and, more specifically, the cubist idea of transparency have been understood primarily through the lens of Colin Rowe and Robert Slutzky's essay 'Transparency: Literal and Phenomenal', first published in 1963.[1] Calling for greater rigour in both the language and formal analysis of contemporary architecture, Rowe and Slutzky set out to distinguish between what they called two 'species' of modernism by clarifying the formal properties of cubist 'transparency'. Taking issue with Sigfried Giedion's comparison in *Space, Time, and Architecture* of

Bauhaus at Dessau,
Walter Gropius and Adolf
Meyer Architects, 1925–26

Walter Gropius's Workshop Building for the Bauhaus at Dessau (1925–26) and Pablo Picasso's painting *L'Arlesienne* of 1912, they sought to supersede the 'evasive' and 'approximate' nature of words such as simultaneity, interpenetration, superimposition, ambivalence and space–time with a formalist notion of phenomenal or seeming transparency. Reworking definitions of transparency taken from György Képes in *Language of Vision* (1944) and László Moholy-Nagy in *Vision in Motion* (1947),[2] they suggested that there was a kind of transparency that was not literal or material but ambiguous – generated by the simultaneous perception of different spatial locations and by superimposed forms that appear to interpenetrate without optically destroying each other.

They suggested that this was comparable to the 'manifold word agglutinations' of James Joyce's puns. The categories of literal and phenomenal transparency were introduced to register this distinction. 'Transparency', they wrote, 'may be an inherent quality of substance – as in a wire mesh or glass curtain wall, or it may be an inherent quality of organisation'.[3]

Taking this opposition as an 'efficient critical instrument', Rowe and Slutzky proceeded to demonstrate the existence of phenomenal transparency in a selection of cubist and post-cubist paintings, notably Fernand Léger's *Three Faces* of 1926, and to observe its absence in a formal model that amalgamated constructivism, expressionism, futurism and De Stijl, represented for them by Moholy-Nagy's *La Sarraz* of 1930. Having taken the notion of phenomenal transparency in part from Moholy's writings, Rowe and Slutzky turned it against him, caustically observing that 'he himself had been unable or unwilling to achieve [it] … in spite of the literal transparency of his paint'.[4] Similarly, they disparaged Giedion's interpretation of cubism in Gropius's Bauhaus as based on the supposed

Rear elevation of the Villa Stein-de Monzie, Le Corbusier, 1926–27

transparency of glass; instead they presented Le Corbusier's Villa Stein-de Monzie at Garches (1926–27) and League of Nations project (1927) as demonstrative of an architecture able to sustain comparison with the striated spatiality of Léger's paradigmatic painting. Culling together formal characteristics from numerous other examples, their elaboration of the opposed categories tended to invert their initial distinction between clarity and ambiguity, commending the specificity of spatial locations in Le Corbusier over the absence of points of reference in Gropius, the assertive corners of the villa at Garches over the dematerialisation of the Bauhaus, and Taut architectonics over walls flowing and blending into one another. By dividing the avant-garde of the early twentieth century into two camps, and arguing that a superior line of development was latent in one in the early transposition of architectonic composition from painting (Cézanne, cubism and purism) into the buildings of Le Corbusier, Rowe and Slutzky effectively undermined the influence of Gropius, Giedion and Moholy-Nagy for architects entering the field in America after 1963.

Subsequent considerations of the relationship between cubism and architecture have tended to orbit around this seminal text, leaving largely unquestioned its theoretical categories and binary logic, as well as its authority as a history of cubism in modern architecture and even its interpretations of Le Corbusier's purism and Gropius's Bauhaus. One notable exception was in 1976 when Manfredo Tafuri and Francesco Dal Co accorded cubism a strategic role in the history of modern architecture without referring to Rowe and Slutzky or their terminology.[5] They presented the earliest cubist paintings of Picasso, Georges Braque and Juan Gris as a historical as well as formal origin for a diverse array of European avant-gardes trying to 'shake off the anxiety provoked by the loss of a center…[in] the chaos of metropolitan formlessness', affirming 'the possibility of a reconquest of the real world'. More than just a point of departure, the revolutionary turn of cubism was, for them, an origin that had already contained its end – the structural characteristics, problematics and flaws of the entire avant-garde project, which they saw played out during the 1920s, especially at the Bauhaus. Tafuri and Dal Co presented the Bauhaus as the 'decantation chamber' and 'refinery' of the avant-gardes in both painting and architecture, striving to achieve a new synthesis that would draw the various post-cubist movements[6] together into a consolidated foundation for reconstructing the world. In this way the antipathy between life and art, art and technology, and deconstruction and construction would be resolved while moving from painting into architecture.

Tafuri and Dal Co outlined a history of artists and architects concerned with the programmatic implications of cubism for modern architecture, one that the other recent

surveys of the period have tended to overlook, but which
Giedion and others had already attempted to represent in
the 1930s and 1940s.[7] Tafuri and Dal Co's account also
implied that the idea of cubism as inaugurating a line of
development not only in art but into architecture had been
introduced not retrospectively by historians but *program-
matically* by avant-garde artists, architects and critics –
including, of course, critic-historians such as Adolf Behne
and Walter Curt Behrendt, as well as Giedion and artists
such as Theo van Doesburg, Kasimir Malevich and El
Lissitzky. Their conceptions of post-cubist art were informed
by their readings in art history and subsequently aimed at
the realisation of a new formal paradigm which would
address issues concerning the built environment. Giedion's
representation of cubism's trajectory into modern architecture, while inadequate to the complexity of this history, is
surprisingly consistent with that of Tafuri and Dal Co,
although he did, as they noted, draw different conclusions.

In this essay I explore how the idea of cubism (which
was itself multiple and contested) was received in architectural discourse in Germany and actively mobilised as both
a point of departure and a goal for a number of influential
figures seeking to overcome what they perceived to be
a loss, not so much of centre, as of unity and synthesis.
In the history thus constructed, relationships among the
avant-garde have assumed a greater complexity than
categories such as expressionism, constructivism and
functionalism have allowed, entailing often perplexing
interweavings of history and theory in art and architecture,
of practices and programmes, complicities, complaints and
misunderstandings. Rivalries between individuals have
come to the fore at the same time as the notion of cubism
has emerged as a common term among formally and
theoretically divergent positions – a term associated with
the widespread belief that the path towards a new architecture began in cubist painting and would end in a new
age that would be the very antithesis of the preceding one:
anti-representational, post-perspectival, abstract and
anti-humanist. In the context of this commonality, differ-

ences and changes in position revolved largely around the problematic relationships between subject and object, identity and otherness, form and formlessness, and construction and destruction. The constitutive instability of these binary oppositions, closely allied with the ongoing destabilisations of modernisation, precluded resolution in formal representations and fuelled the restless uncertainty and experimentalism of the avant-garde in the early years of the Weimar period.

Within this territory, I present three independent yet overlapping stories, focusing in turn on the critic Adolf Behne, on Walter Gropius and the early Bauhaus, and on Sigfried Giedion. Provoked by the architecture of Czech cubism in 1914, Behne began to formulate a programmatic conception of cubism as a revolutionary anti-classical and anti-European worldview. In 1919, he published a strident manifesto for cubist architecture based on the idea that purified artistic means (construction rather than imitation) would facilitate open and unpredetermined creative production, which he conceived as a kind of passage from the immaterial realm of the suprahuman into the material sphere of humanity through the activity of construction. For this he combined preoccupations of expressionism and so-called German cubism with aspects of Paul Scheerbart's utopian fantasy of glass architecture, a combination that crystallised in a notion of utopian cubist images. While Behne's association with Bruno Taut is well known, the implications of his vision for Walter Gropius and the early Bauhaus have been less studied. Their importance, however, is underscored by the fact that Behne began to criticise expressionism as early as 1918 and progressively distanced himself from Taut after joining Gropius in the leadership of the Workers' Council for Art in 1919.

The complexity of this episode is compounded by the influence of De Stijl – itself divided after 1921 when Theo van Doesburg and JJP Oud split over the correct interpretation of cubism for architecture – and then constructivism, particularly in relation to László Moholy-Nagy, whose artistic research into transparency, central to

his teaching at the Bauhaus, was itself inspired by Behne's
call in 1919 for a Scheerbartian cubism. Although he did
not refer to Behne, Gideon's notion of construction as
an automatic writing of the subconscious implicitly took
up Behne's earlier interpretation of cubism, but was
distinguished from it by incorporating a phenomenology
of perception that Gideon attempted to articulate with the
idea of space–time taken from both scientific and artistic
theory. His later reading of the Bauhaus as the first
realisation of cubist space–time in architecture was offered,
then, in the context of a broad spectrum of post-cubist
research into the implications for architecture of modern
painting (De Stijl, constructivism and purism). It should
also be understood in the context of claims made in the
late 1920s that the Bauhaus building at Dessau marked the
beginning of a widely disseminated glass architecture,
anticipated initially in utopian dreams of a crystalline
cubism that would break with the legacy of Renaissance
perspective and anthropomorphism.

ADOLF BEHNE'S OPENNESS: CONSTRUCTION AND IMMANENCE

From 1914 the critic Adolf Behne, still working within
the early discourse of expressionism, began to appreciate
cubism for its purification of the means of artistic
expression into an elemental, primitive and architectonic
language capable of expanding the world of human
experience beyond what he took to be the limitations of
humanist anthropomorphism. Behne's gradual embrace
of cubism was prompted less by French cubism, or even its
German variations by Franz Marc, Lyonel Feininger or
Paul Klee, than by the arrival of Czech cubism in Herwarth
Walden's Sturm gallery and magazine in Berlin during
1913–14.[8] It was informed not only by the literature on
French cubist painting (especially Albert Gleizes and Jean
Metzinger's essay of 1912)[9] but also by articles from the
young Czech architect Vlastislav Hofman and the artist

Josef Čapek, editor of the periodical of the Group of
Plastic Artists.

Reiterating the idea of modern art as an art of form,
colour and space akin to music, Hofman's 'Der Geist der
Umwandlung in der bildenden Kunst', published in
December 1913,[10] emphasised the impulse to organise and
overcome a reality perceived to be formless and indifferent
by pursuing both the idealisation of form as the thing-in-
itself and the logic of artistic fabrication – turning from the
exterior to the interior of reality, to its very skeleton.
Likening the cubists' dismantling of space to the out-
stretching of wings preparing 'for the most daring flight',
Hofman concluded that the modern world demanded
something more elementary and fundamental than comfort
and illusion: it demanded its own construction. This idea of
modern art as an art of construction was taken up by Bruno
Taut in his essay 'Eine Notwendigkeit' of February 1914, in
which he warned (perhaps with Czech cubism in mind)
against architecture taking over the external forms of
painting. Rather he suggested that 'architecture was by its
very nature cubist', was already free of perspective and
need not limit itself to cubism's angular forms.[11] His own
recent projects – the skeletal Monument of Iron in Leipzig
of 1913 and the elemental facade of his Hardenbergstrasse
apartment block in Berlin in 1911–12 – were subsequently
reviewed by Behne precisely in terms of such *sachlich*
autonomous forms.[12]

Josef Čapek's essay of May 1914, 'Moderne Architektur',[13] contributed the idea that the transposition of cubism
from art into architecture was occurring in phases analogous to those of cubism in art. Disparaging architecture's
lifeless performance relative to the discoveries of cubist
paintings, which he called a new spatial-sculptural
presentation of things aimed at the sublime, he insisted on
the need to take cubism beyond the application of jagged
and crooked motifs on traditional architectural elements –
the discipline of architecture had to be transformed from
the ground up. Čapek suggested that the first stage in
developing the architectural equivalent of cubist painting,

like the first stage of French cubism, had already been superseded by the 'latest architecture' just as the later experiments of Picasso had led to a stronger synthetic cubism. He characterised this process as transforming the linear spatial net or geometric skeleton of the earlier efforts into a pre-architectonic language, a medium itself full of meaning. The 'mysterious autonomy' and 'incalculable instinctive logic' of this new architecture was distinguished by what he saw as its intelligent translation of inner movement and plasticity into the outer physiognomy of the building, like the functional and formal definition of a machine. While he did not give examples, the structural conception of cubism in the work of the young Hofman, exploring skeletal expression and cellular aggregation, does appear radically different, for instance, from Josef Gocár's 1911 Tychonova Street houses in Prague. Čapek's emphasis on the contributions yet to be made by the younger generation, along with the numerous affinities in their theoretical dispositions, must surely have stimulated the young architects and critics of the Sturm circle.

In December 1914, Behne began to draw a distinction between expressionism and cubism that is conceptually similar to Čapek's distinction between early and later cubisms. In his opening remarks for an exhibition of 'Deutsche Expressionisten' at Walden's gallery, and in an almost concurrent article on 'Expressionistische Architektur', Behne began by replaying the familiar opposition of expressionism to impressionism, considered in the broadest sense as worldviews that subsumed art, literature and architecture.[14] Where impressionism had been satisfied with the surface impression of appearance, Behne suggested that the meaning of expressionism lay in its desire to express or materialise the 'spiritual quintessence of experience'. Citing the German Gothic as precedent, Behne took expressionist art to signal the return of true artistic work, understood as allowing spiritual things to 'arise' and 'grow organically' through artistic fantasy and creativity rather than being 'constructed like machines'. For the artists featured,[15] and for the architects Adolf Loos and

Bruno Taut, whose expressionism he contrasted to the impressionism of Richard Riemerschmidt and Ludwig Hoffmann, 'the means for the achievement of this goal was cubism'. While Behne considered cubism as potentially a cold and intellectual method, it was not 'a dumb kind of stylisation'. Rather 'cubism means that which for the construction of form makes possible the crystallisation of expression due to a distant similarity of geometries'. Artists were cubists because 'there are certain things that can only be spoken in this language'. The fact that Behne felt no need to describe this new language indicates the extent to which, by then, the very notion of cubism as the new, pure, elemental, geometric and autonomous language of pictorial construction – in Franz Marc's words, of 'mystic inner construction' – had become a staple of German artistic discourse.[16]

Behne's distinction between natural, organic growth and mechanical repetition was drawn from the biologist Jakob von Uexküll, whose book *Bausteine zu einer biologische Weltanschauung*[17] he discussed in detail in 'Biologie und Kubismus', an article of September 1915. It was in this essay that his emphasis, and the formal attributes previously associated with expressionism, shifted to cubism. Behne recounted Uexküll's contention that all living beings exist in two worlds: the perceptible world (*Merkwelt*) of knowable, physical, chemical nature which is experienced by beings and is the world of human technical capability, and a larger world of mysterious and fundamentally unknowable life (*Wirkungswelt*). For Uexküll, every living thing exists in both, forming its own world picture (*Weltbild*) from a specific standpoint within an immense ambiguity and flux. Not all world pictures, Behne continued, operate in the same way in relation to the larger domain of life and life-forces. Some – he cited naturalism and impressionism in the arts – were considered to take a fixed standpoint outside the body and outside events, the standpoint of perspective. Behne took architecture guided by perspective to be more limiting than the building art of 'truly creative' historic periods, unconstrained by such a representational grid. The cubist world-feeling, he explained, knows nothing of the fixed point of orientation and detests atmospheric evaporation. While he took the standpoint of cubism to be ambiguous, he considered its discoveries to be profound. While its elements were thought to be fundamental, pure and clear, its totality was in flux and unfixed. Where Uexküll, in Behne's view, mistakenly supported the 'half-new, decorative art' of the *Brücke* (including Erich Heckel, Ernst Ludwig Kirchner and Max Pechstein), Behne argued that the true new art was to be found in the cubist works of Robert Delaunay, Franz Marc, Carl Mense, Fernand Léger, Marc Chagall, Oskar Kokoschka and Jacoba van Heemskerck:

Cubism does not want a banal description of the psychological meaning of bodies and events from a specific external standpoint, rather it wants life itself! The cubist artist is in the middle of things, they surround him, their abundance brings him happiness, their never-resting, ever-moving, puzzling, autonomous life is like an intoxication. No positivistic result, no explanation, no moral and no application or lesson – rather glorification, admiration, adoration.[18]

Behne argued that while representations of the larger effective world *Merkwelt* are not possible as such – all efforts simply reproduce the conditions of human bodies, senses and cognitive faculties – it is nevertheless possible, through art, to give form to this feeling for life. He considered it the task of art, more specifically the task of cubism, to expand the perceptible world by making the feeling for life visible.[19]

Although prior to the war Behne had joined the circle around Walden, publishing articles and even his first book with him,[20] in 1918 he was writing against the 'bourgeois' art dealer, despite Walden's central role in promoting the new 'revolutionary' artists of Europe. In the wake of expressionism's first financial success during the wartime art boom of 1917 and the growing politicisation of the

Berlin avant-garde following the October Revolution in Russia, Behne attacked what he called the co-opted pseudo-revolutionary art associated with Walden's Sturm as 'an art of luxury and pleasure [that] wants isolation, the unconnectedness of art, assails the joining of art and life... and yet does everything humanly possible to meld this art intimately with the better middle class'.[21] Instead, Behne proposed a cubist art distinguished by its 'constructive' relationship to the world.[22] 'The cubist', he wrote, 'strives for more than pure painting and pure sculpture. Beyond all concern for method and system, he participates in building the world'. For this reason Behne saw architecture, drawing all the other arts under its wing, as both necessary and exemplary for the full realisation of cubism as a world-making art (*Weltkunst*). Walden's reply, when it finally came in 1919, resisted the assimilation of fine art to architecture and ridiculed Behne's interpretation of cubism as an activity of building (*bauen*).[23]

The conception of cubism as a pure, biological and intuitive constructive activity became central to Behne's 1919 *Die Wiederkehr der Kunst*, in which he turned the metaphor of cubism as language into the idea of a direct and unmediated construction, 'an unfabricated fabrication' free of a priori conventions and dogmas. Through true building (*bauen*) Behne believed that creative fantasy could materialise the feeling of life, which was the hallmark of true art – not as 'a language of forms' or 'a specific body of learning' but as something more 'fundamental', the 'true reality' and 'Absolute!'[24] His examples now broadened to include 'the free, new and self-evident constructions of India',[25] the naive art of children and primitives, and the self-effacing transcendentalism of the East, contrasted with the anthropomorphic projection of European classicism, technology and perspective. He distinguished periods of true European art (Gothic and romantic) from periods in which art was eclipsed by classicism and naturalism. In short, he argued that the cubist revolution was displacing Western humanism, creating a greater openness to the nonhuman, pre-human and even inhuman.[26] Behne held that humanity could not be the measure of all things, because it was not a closed unity but a world system, both infinite in itself and set within an always greater and more comprehensive world-being.[27] His programme for social reform flowed from cubism's artistic mandate – to 'free itself from the Greek man-measure' in order to 'change the European',[28] not through evolution but by clearing a space (elemental and impoverished) in which true art could arise by itself, mediated only by the purest of means. By invoking cubism's potential to create a revolution in the history of art and the quality of latency, immanence or arising possessed by cubist images,[29] Behne attempted to express a distinctive vision of the future within the avant-garde's rhetoric of 'new beginnings' – common to both expressionists and Dadaists – which assumed increasing urgency at the close of the war, not only in the arts but in all spheres of German life.[30]

The hallmark of Behne's cubism was its 'architectonic' character, which he described as a hidden striving for unity, bound to the body of the star earth, and beyond ego, place and time.[31] He offered no description of cubism's formal properties, for this would have wrongly privileged external appearances. Instead, what he called cubism may be understood as the striving of humanity to expand its own limited domain in order to materialise something of the formless unity of the cosmos. Yet Behne's revised list of cubists in 1919 gives some indication of the kind of work he had in mind, emphasising Carl Mense, Frits Stuckenberg, Arnold Topp and 'especially' Lyonel Feininger:

I find that architectonic, which I previously identified as a secret urge to a final unity, in the pictures of these cubists, among which the sculptures of Alexander Archipenko should be included. Today painting really gives us great hope that the goal of unity will be achieved in the art that should actually lead: architecture. A call then goes out to all young architects to make their contribution so that architecture can emerge from its current impasse.[32]

With this call in mind, Behne promoted the role of architecture in the reform programmes of the Worker's Council for Art and introduced the 'German cubist' Feininger to Gropius, who responded to his transparent crystallisations of landscapes and cities by appointing him the first new 'master of form' in painting at the Bauhaus.[33]

However, no sooner had Behne put forward the idea that cubism began in painting than he countered it with the proposition that it had actually begun in literature with Paul Scheerbart's 1889 novel *Paradies*, which he called 'the first, purest, and clearest, the more universal and so far unbroken articulation of our will'. Concerned that cubism in painting could easily be misunderstood as just another way to make pictures interesting, Behne suggested that painting was simply where the 'inner transformation of art', already evident less visibly in other places, was first recognised by the public.[34] In assimilating Scheerbart to his conception of cubism, Behne's argument became utopian in a double sense. It assumed epochal dimensions by linking the inauguration of a new era in art – 'cubism is what we make it … it lies in the future'[35] – first to Uexküll's theory of passage or materialisation from the effective to the perceptible world, and then to Scheerbart's utopian vision of *Glass Architecture* (1914), capable of overcoming materiality, producing non-human effects and transforming Europeans into a new kind of people through a 'spiritual revolution'.[36] Under the sign of a Scheerbartian cubism capable of fulfilling the potentiality of industrial technology as well as a cubist art (a combination that Giedion would later reiterate), Behne saw true art returning 'like the sun coming out behind the clouds' of humanist classicism.[37]

Higher truths, Behne continued, cannot be grasped through reason but only through fantasy.[38] With this in mind, he called the utopian fantasy drawings by Bruno Taut for his Alpine architecture a 'spiritual reality, not an ideal project'.[39] Yet in focusing on Scheerbart's architectural fantasies, even more than Taut's, Behne underscored his interpretation of the cubist image as the purest possible expression of utopia, seemingly even less encumbered in the abstract realm of words than in painting or architecture. It was to satisfy the urgent desire at the close of the war for utopian images manifesting spiritual reality that the radical left Workers' Council for Art (led by Gropius and Behne) organised the 'Exhibition of Unknown Architects' in April 1919, deliberately featuring works by non-architects – artists and others uncontaminated by architectural learning or training.[40]

Among the various participants, Gropius singled out the works by young Russian Jefim Golyscheff – composer and musical child genius, maker of instruments and children's toys, who had then arrived in the world of the Berlin avant-garde and collaborated with the dadaists on their first exhibition, held (like the 'Exhibition of Unknown Architects') at IB Neumann's Graphisches Kabinett. Gropius called Golyscheff's drawings 'extreme examples of what we want: utopia'. In an article on his work, Behne stressed the importance of contributions by the untrained, by children, primitive 'barbarians' and proletarians. Despairing of how learning inhibits 'holy merriment', he described Golyscheff's ability to lose himself as a prerequisite for a new beginning, the 'zero point' from which 'the play impulse of the child to begin again goes forth'.[41] Although criticised by the older generation of expressionists, Behne defended Golyscheff's 'renewal of art' and warned that expressionism risked falling asleep. He insisted that many generations would still need to destroy and build again, just as the expressionists had done. In this spirit, he also criticised the Dadaists as just another 'ism' and cited Golyscheff's flyer 'A-ismus' in order to explain that Golyscheff had broken his affiliation with Dada, wanting simply to become an atom, to give himself over just like a child, to create with primitive pleasure. The bright pieces of his collages struck Behne as having nothing in them of the expressionist hankering for soulfulness; rather they 'bring – as small as they are! – greetings from the greater world!' With Golyscheff, Behne's cubist return of art assumed the character of a continuous cultural revolution – 'never a fixed state' but always new. The idea of cubism as an origin had become unhitched from the quest for a new style; instead it now inaugurated an era characterised by ceaseless inaugurations, destroying and building again and again in the unending pleasure, even intoxication, of (godlike) creation.[42]

BAUHAUS *GESTALTUNG*: PAINTERLY AND FUNCTIONAL

Fortified by the hopeful images of otherworldly and unprecedented utopias, Gropius moved quickly from image to embodiment; before the end of the year he had taken charge of the Bauhaus, formulated its new educational programme, hired his first teachers and reopened his practice with Adolf Meyer. While in April he had admired images of utopia, by December he was reluctant to join Taut's Crystal Chain and did not contribute to their correspondence or their 'Neues Bauen' exhibition of May 1920. Behne likewise declined to participate in the Chain, and while he still supported them he also continued to distance himself from expressionism in his writings.[43] During the winter of 1921–22 he publicly turned against 'the wave of utopianism and romanticism'.[44] By October 1922 he had even turned against Bruno Taut, whose work he had championed since 1914 but whose programme of painting building facades in Magdeburg he now criticised, calling instead for the use of colour as an integral property of materials.[45]

However, like Gropius's more celebrated turn from expressionism to De Stijl and constructivist functionalism, Behne's critique of visionary utopianism should not be construed as a sudden change of heart about expression-ism, for this had begun much earlier and was, in fact, consistent throughout his writings from 1918 onwards. Despite his support of Taut in those years, Behne's pro-grammatic conception of cubism distinguishes his own position even then. Privately, Behne had already distanced himself from aspects of *Wiederkehr* in October 1920, when, in a letter to his new friend the Dutch architect JJP Oud, he wrote: 'To start, let me say … that I began writing the book more than two years ago. It emerged in the deepest depression of war duty in a military hospital and in the hope that there would be a saving revolution. Today, I would change many things.'[46] Having turned his eye to Russia after 1917 and then to Holland, where the revolutionary aspirations for the new art and architecture were being advanced while Germany was still at war, Behne had little patience for the arbitrariness, obscurity and marginality of expressionism in Germany. 'From the periphery, on whose rim paper pagodas for no one had been mounted, one turned to the centre.'[47]

In Holland Behne discovered not only De Stijl but within it another perspective on the relationship of cubism to architecture. In an essay begun in 1916, Oud and Theo van Doesburg – the driving force behind De Stijl and pan-avant-gardists *par excellence* – had speculated on the implications for architecture of ideas initiated in cubist painting, which the De Stijl group sought to extend. Over the following five years they pursued this goal in theoretical writings and experimental collaborations on architectural projects that used colour, contrast and pattern in ways informed by van Doesburg's analytical sketches, paintings and stained glass. The most celebrated of these projects was De Vonk (1917–18), a seaside hostel for young women, which featured vibrant and oscillating tile floors and wall mosaics designed by van Doesburg. In the early issues of the journal *De Stijl*, Oud presented theoretical projects clearly influenced by the cubic massing and geometric plans of Frank Lloyd Wright, which he associated with this cubist-inspired research in architecture.

Despite their long-standing association, van Doesburg parted company with Oud in the fall of 1921, when the architect criticised the colour scheme he had proposed for a large housing project in Rotterdam.[48] Van Doesburg had intended to dissolve the mass of Oud's brick building by applying vertical stripes of bright colours in a rhythmic pattern, just as he had dissolved the naturalistic contours of human figures and animals into compositions of elemental geometry and colour, in keeping with his conception of cubism as the expression of space through the mathematical purification of form.[49] In an exchange of articles that followed their split, each reaffirmed the ideal of cubism in architecture, which had been the strategic point of departure for their research into elementarism,[50] but with the painter asserting that colour was the primary medium even for architecture while the architect insisted on a builderly and social understanding of the medium – rationalist, constructivist and functionalist rather than abstract; cognisant of social needs, materials and modes of production as well as colour.[51] For Oud, to achieve pure and elemental architectonic means did not require the elimination of closure or the dissolution of materiality 'once and for all'. Nor did he consider cubism itself to be the coming style, but regarded it as merely a transition that once completed would give way to the 'new style'.

At the heart of the dispute between van Doesburg and Oud was the question of how to transpose cubist formlessness correctly so as to produce an architecture of open forms comparable to the painterly dissolution of objects in cubism.[52] The introduction of ideas concerning open forms, formlessness and painterliness was informed by van Doesburg's reading of Heinrich Wölfflin's *Kunstgeschichtliche Grundbegriffe* (1915), and the debate between van Doesburg and Oud was marked by the binary categories of Wölfflin's theory of stylistic change. For Wölfflin, the history of art oscillated between opposed psychologies of form and modalities of vision – linear and painterly, closed and open compositions, planar and recessional perceptual effects, tectonic and atectonic form, the solid figure and its appearance, enduring form and movement, the thing-in-itself and the thing in its relations, death and life. Van Doesburg fully embraced the idea of movement as the subject of painting not in the futurists' sense of depicting a moving subject, but in the cubists' sense of the whole canvas in motion.[53] Oud, on the other hand, affirmed the ideal of a nonacademic classicism in which form was the purest possible expression of the life of the object or building. He interpreted the idea of formlessness in architecture within the framework of HP Berlage's rationalism as simply opposed to formalism and the use of predetermined forms. For Oud – whose affinity with Behne becomes clear on this point – architecture was formless when each new building and each new form emerged into being without preconception, as a unique and pure presence. He called this organic–mechanic cubism an 'unhistorical classicism', taking purity to be its hallmark.

Beginning in 1919, Behne and Feininger served as the principal intermediaries between the Dutch and the Bauhaus. Behne's widely distributed 'Call' on behalf of the Workers' Council for Art was published in *De Stijl* in September 1919, while one of Feininger's paintings was included in the November issue, together with an appreciation by van Doesburg.[54] Holland became Behne's first foreign destination after the war, in the summer of 1920, and following his trip he praised the new Dutch architecture in numerous articles, started a lasting friendship with Oud, and arranged the first meeting between van Doesburg and Gropius in December 1920, the day after the completion ceremony of Gropius and Adolf Meyer's wooden 'block' house for the industrialist Alfred Sommerfeld.[55] Van Doesburg almost immediately moved to Weimar, where he stayed for about two years, hopeful of a teaching appointment that never materialised. He nevertheless attempted to influence the school of Gropius, criticising its embrace of handicraft rather than machine production and its promotion of free individual expression over the collective refashioning of reality. Regardless of the appropriateness of these critiques, he was, consequently, quick to claim credit for Gropius's celebrated turn from the so-called expressionism of the Sommerfeld House to the theatre at Jena.[56]

Although van Doesburg's characterisation of the Sommerfeld House as expressionist continues to be reiterated even today, it was overly dependent on his prior critique of expressionist art and simply turned the terms of that critique on Gropius's architecture. Yet a consideration of the house in relation to expressionist art remains inadequate to its rich, ambiguous and strange mixture of forms – recalling works by Frank Lloyd Wright, primitive vernaculars both European and non-European, the English arts and crafts movement, and formal motifs from Czech cubism (notably the prismatic windows and entry and the scalloped roof, proposed but not executed), as well as the crystalline geometries of architectonic fantasies by many of the artists singled out by Behne as exemplary Scheerbartian cubists. Considered in terms of such an expanded field of affinities, the house may be understood as a synthetic quest for primary architectonic ur-forms, informed by Behne's case for a primitive architectonic cubism with which the critic had already identified Gropius, as well as Henry van de Velde and Bruno Taut. Prompted by the furniture in Gropius's Berlin apartment in 1919 – pieces by van de Velde and a 'zigzag' sofa – Golyscheff had certainly encouraged Gropius 'to be cubist rather than cubic … to unfold all sides'.[57]

Similarly, van Doesburg's claim to have influenced the design of the Jena theatre, while undoubtedly of consequence,[58] has tended to obscure Gropius and Meyer's long-standing use of generative geometries, which they learned from Peter Behrens and, in the case of Meyer, also from the Dutch architect JLM Lauweriks, who had joined Behrens's School of Decorative Arts in Düsseldorf at the recommendation of Oud's mentor, HP Berlage.[59] As a student there Meyer had learned Lauweriks' method of designing based on a geometrical grid, evolved through subdivision and multiplication of a square with an inscribed circle. Lauweriks hoped that the grid would provide an underlying architectonic system capable of drawing every aspect of design, from the site plan to the furniture, into a single unified structure – an idea that Behne identified as crucial to the architectonics of cubism. One of Meyer's student designs was even singled out by Berlage in a published lecture concerning the use of geometry as the basis for a new architecture, finally free of the need to imitate historical styles.[60]

Not only did Meyer continue to use geometric design principles in the work of the Gropius office – in the relentlessly cubic Jena theatre as well as in the open geometries of the prismatic Kallenbach House project of 1922 – he also taught geometric composition in his architecture course at the Bauhaus. Moreover, this interest in the geometric design processes intersected not only with the common German interpretation of cubism as a geometric art, but also with an appreciation of Wright's architecture, which Gropius and Meyer studied carefully for their own work both before and after the war.[61] Oud also considered Wright important, not only for his theoretical projects but as an influence across European modernism that he associated, at first, with cubism. By the mid-1920s, however, Oud expressed concern over the prevalence of a Wrightian formalism and instead promoted European cubism, which he now insisted had developed independently of Wright's influence – 'a first run at a new synthesis of form, a new unhistorical classicism' that still held the greatest promise for the future of architecture.[62]

Oud's significance for Gropius and his partner Meyer may be seen in their response to his lecture of February 1921, 'On the Future Art of Building and Its Architectonic Possibilities'. Meyer in particular was so struck by it that he initiated a correspondence with Oud and arranged for its translation and publication in Bruno Taut's periodical *Frühlicht*.[63] In the lecture, Oud developed his programme for a new architecture based on a materialist conception of the discipline and its social purposes but striving to overcome them for spiritual effects, the terms of which already articulated the criteria for his subsequent critique of van Doesburg's colour scheme. While van Doesburg was eventually rebuffed by Gropius, Oud was asked to lecture during the Bauhaus week. Moreover, when Behne and Moholy-Nagy organised the small competition for the design of the Kallenbach House, they invited Oud to participate along with Gropius and Meyer, and Hilberseimer. Although Oud's design remained unexecuted, it influenced subsequent projects by Gropius and Meyer, leading them in the direction of a functional and constructive (in his terms, 'classical') openness rather than the geometric openness that they attempted with the rotated and broken cubes of their project for the Kallenbachs, its site plan a unified structure of inner and outer space rendered as a field of oscillating primary colours.[64] Their approach to the colour scheme for the Jena theatre – its porches blue, its foyer light yellow, cloakrooms violet, staircases terracotta and auditorium salmon pink, grey and deep blue[65] – was also closer to Oud's use of colour as a means of articulating spatial and architectural elements than it was to van Doesburg's dissolving of substance. And finally, anticipating the critique of formalism levelled against both van Doesburg and the early Bauhaus, Gropius – following suggestions in Oud's 1921 lecture – shifted his programme on the occasion of the Bauhaus exhibition to the quest for a new 'synthesis of art and technology', for which the Bauhaus became internationally celebrated.

Van Doesburg, on the other hand, renewed his quest for the architecture of De Stijl by collaborating with the young architect Cornelis van Eesteren, whom he had met when van Eesteren was a student in Weimar. Using colour once more to contrast, dissolve and mitigate the closed form of three projects for Léonce Rosenberg's De Stijl show in Paris in 1923, van Doesburg finally achieved the breakthrough to which he aspired. By colouring the surfaces of van Eesteren's axonometric drawings, he discovered that the closed mass of the building could be elementalised into homogeneous immaterial planes and opened up, thereby transforming cubic blocks into formless, open crystalline configurations of interpenetrating planes, which van Doesburg thought of in terms of space–time. This process of abstraction was pushed even further in van Doesburg's counter-reliefs of transparent as well as coloured planes, which Giedion later called 'a vision of space'.[66] In 1925, van Doesburg's theory of planes, colours, lines, volumes, space and time as the elementary means of architectural expression or *Gestaltung* (form creation) was published in the Bauhaus book series overseen by Moholy-Nagy. Here, van

Doesburg emphasised the important proposition – first propagated by the formalist theorist Konrad Fiedler in the late nineteenth century[67] – that an observer's experience of an artwork constituted a re-enactment of form creation in the consciousness of the observer.[68]

Ironically, just as Behne turned from the most radically utopian aspects of his programme, his image of an architectonic and crystalline cubism inspired yet another line of experimentation by Moholy-Nagy, hired by Gropius in 1923 to replace Johannes Itten in the strategic preliminary course at the Bauhaus. Having arrived in Berlin in early 1920, Moholy took up the idea of glass architecture to refer to his work during 1921 and 1922, prompted less by Bruno Taut than by the interpretations of Scheerbart by Behne and the dadaists, who also claimed him as their spiritual father.[69] He applied the title to works based on colour and overlapping geometric form charged with depth and drawn mechanically to eliminate the hand of the artist – elemental compositions influenced also by Kasimir Malevich's suprematist paintings. Unlike the dadaists, however, Moholy pursued the cause of liberation through the creative rather than destructive capacity of the artist. He believed in the need for a new order based on rationality, the wonder of technology, and the discovery of natural laws of construction and vision. The disembodied utopia of glass architecture, unrealised and unrealisable as yet, continued to inform his work as he explored qualities of transparency and interpretation, not only in paintings, lithographs and woodcuts but also in mechanical means of reproduction – photographs, photomontages, photographs and films – and in designs for stage sets and exhibitions through which he approached architecture more directly. Like Malevich, El Lissitzky and László Peri, Moholy understood the project of modern art as beginning in painting, more specifically cubism, but aiming for a new architecture – a trajectory registered clearly in his book of 1929, *Von Material zu Architektur*, in which he summarised his teaching at the Bauhaus.[70]

Transparency (*Durchsichtigkeit*) and interpenetration

(*Durchdringung*, connoting also fusion and consciousness) became the strategic properties of Moholy's post-cubist conception of architecture encapsulated in the idea of space as *Raumgestaltung* (space creation), which he developed together with his close friend Sigfried Giedion and made the central topic of his book of 1929. Travelling through France in the summer of 1925, Moholy and Giedion – together with the photographer Lucia Moholy and the art historian Carola Giedion-Welcker – discovered the pleasures of the new spatial culture in the open structure of the Eiffel Tower in Paris. Two years later, Giedion pointed to the Pont Transbordeur in Marseilles as another early precursor of the avant-garde of the 1920s and was the first to publish (Moholy-inspired) photographs of it.[71] The final section of Moholy's book, in which he compiles a panoramic portrait of *Raumgestaltung* as evidenced in contemporary industrial structures, urban landscapes and set designs, as well as in Le Corbusier's Villas La Roche-Jeanneret (1923) and Gropius's Bauhaus building (1925–26), complemented Giedion's history of modern construction in his 1928 *Bauen in Frankreich*. With abstracted close-up photographs by Gotthardt Itting and Lux Feininger (son of Lyonel), Moholy presented the Bauhaus building as an exemplar of how 'inside and outside interpenetrate one another' in the reflections and transparencies of its glass walls – the tenuous surface into which the boundary between inside and out had dissolved. These would become precisely the terms for Giedion's interpretation of the Bauhaus as cubist.

The final images of *Von Material zu Architektur* are especially revealing of Moholy's new vision of architecture as the non-substantial or virtual generation of spatial and volumetric configurations: Itting's almost unrecognisable close-up of the Bauhaus at the virtual intersection of the glazed bridge with the glazed entrance, seen from above as if hovering in space; a view from below looking up at workers scrambling across the steel skeleton of a new planetarium, suspended in the transparent net like 'a formation of airplanes in the ether'; and, lastly, another

exposure by Jan Kamman of the van Nelle factory in
Rotterdam by Brinkman and van der Vlugt, entitled simply
'architecture'. The caption reads: 'From two superimposed
photographs (negatives) emerges the illusion of spatial
interpenetration, which only the next generation will be
able to experience as reality – as glass architecture'.[72]

Moholy was not alone, however, during the late
1920s, in still thinking of glass architecture, and especially
Gropius's Bauhaus, in terms of Scheerbart's and Behne's
utopias. In an article of 1926 on the properties, potentials
and technical developments of glass construction, illustrated with Itting's photograph of the Bauhaus, Gropius
himself linked the newly completed Bauhaus to Scheerbart's vision when he wrote that 'glass architecture, which
was just a poetic utopia not long ago, now becomes reality
without constraint'.[73] Also in 1926, Arthur Korn introduced
his picture book, *Glas im Bau und als Gebrauchsgegenstand*,
by suggesting that a 'new glass age has begun which is
equal in beauty to the old of Gothic windows …[that]
afforded glimpses of paradise in luminous colours'.[74] It
was the special characteristic of glass, he went on, that it
is 'noticeable yet not quite visible. It is the great membrane,
full of mystery, delicate yet tough. It can enclose and open
up spaces in more than one direction. Its peculiar advan-
tage is in the diversity of the impressions it creates'. He too
turned to Gropius's Bauhaus – particularly to a photograph
by Lucia Moholy – to illustrate his contention that 'the
visible depth behind the thin skin of glass is the exciting
factor'. It was this same photograph, accompanied with
similar observations about the enticements of glass, that
Giedion later made famous in comparing it to Picasso's
cubist *L'Arlesienne*.

SIGFRIED GIEDION'S TRANSPARENCY:
ART AND ARCHITECTURE

Considered within the long history of *Space, Time, and
Architecture*, Giedion's comparison between Picasso's

painting of 1912 and Gropius and Meyer's building of 1926 offered evidence of the historical progression from painting into architecture at the same time as it exemplified the new formal paradigm for what Giedion called the 'contemporary image' in art and 'open construction' in architecture. In describing the value for architecture of cubist research into the representational space, Giedion made the technological character of this development explicit and even illustrated it graphically in a two-page spread. Beginning with a cubist collage by Georges Braque of 1913, Giedion's arrow of history proceeded to an undated neo-plastic painting by Piet Mondrian, followed by one of Kasimir Malevich's suprematist *Architectons* and by the unbuilt house for Léonce Rosenburg by van Doesburg and Cornelis van Eesteren ('the effect is as if the blind surfaces of the Malevich sculpture had suddenly received sight').[75] The trajectory here culminated in the fully realised architecture of the Bauhaus at Dessau, 'the only large building of its date which was so complete a crystallisation of the new space conception'.[76] While Giedion's linear sequence imposed an order and hierarchy on projects that were in fact parallel experiments – suprematism, De Stijl, purism and the Bauhaus – he did so by drawing on their parallel self-conceptions as moving from painting toward architecture. For Giedion, following Malevich, van Doesburg and Le Corbusier, this necessarily entailed rationalisation in order to correct the 'aberrations' of cubism.[77]

In addition, Giedion used the history internal to modern art as parallel to the history of architecture over a much longer time. Picasso had already been invoked when Giedion juxtaposed his sculpted *Head* of 1910 with the baroque cupola of Francesco Borromini's mid-seventeenth-century Sant'Ivo in Rome, claiming that each bore evidence of a new feeling for interconnecting interior and exterior space – a feeling struggling for its own expression, still constrained within old conceptions of bodies and buildings as closed forms. From this beginning, Giedion traced the various paths through which the modern space conception – which he called 'space–time', citing the poet Guillaume

Apollinaire and the non-Euclidean mathematician
Hermann Minkowski[78] – emerged into consciousness from
within the perspectival conception of space inaugurated
in the Renaissance. Although he emphasised the 'optical
revolution' of cubism over futurism's inconclusive research
into space–time, Giedion regretted that futurism had
been cut short by the loss of its key figures during the war.
He acknowledged the importance of this work for
reconsidering the status of the object in terms of time and
a new plasticity – as perpetually in a state of motion.

Giedion treated space–time, like perspective before
it, as a structuring condition or informing principle that
defined the consciousness of the era and regulated not only
art but also architecture, gardens and cities – the entire
spatial world of humanity.[79] In contrast to the limited
representational and experiential possibilities of perspective,
he presented it as an expanded optical and spatial realm, one
of excited emotions, greater freedom and enhanced
participation by the observer. Unlike perspective, however,
space–time could not be represented in a diagram of lines
or forms, since it was in fact contingent on the active subject
moving in space and time, contingent on phenomenology of
perception as well as production, signified by the notions of
Gestaltung and *Raumgestaltung*. In *Bauen in Frankreich*, Giedion
had already used the idea of *Gestaltung* to refer to the
productivity of the subconscious manifesting the impulses
of life in constructions that used the new synthetic materials
of iron, glass and concrete.[80]

In keeping with the notion of *Gestaltung* and theories
of *Raumgestaltung* (from the historical August Schmarsow
to Moholy-Nagy),[81] Giedion considered the viewer as actively
re-experiencing the formation of buildings and spaces,
albeit in cognitive rather than strictly material terms. The
expansion of experience made possible by the fluidity and
openness of this condition was seen as exemplary of
modernity. As he made clear in his descriptions of the
Bauhaus and the Villa Savoye, buildings in space–time can
only be comprehended by an observer moving all around
them, inside and out, up and down. Their identities as

objects remain necessarily incomplete, indeterminate and contingent on the plastic process of space creation grasped through the apperception of partial perspectives integrated over time. In Giedion's conception of space–time, static forms and elements became support for the endless and endlessly varied activity of creating space in the fourth dimension.

Just as he traced the history of spatial and temporal research in the visual arts, so in the realm of building science Giedion tracked the gradual emergence, self-determination and refinement of technical forms such as the steel frame, the reinforced concrete slab and the suspended plane of the curtain wall. However, what gave cubism its special significance for Giedion was that with it the plane came into consciousness as a constituent element of pictorial construction, while the parallel development of the slab in engineering took place unconsciously. It was consequently the role of architects (as artist-constructors) to make this into a self-reflective means of expression.

Giedion's selection of Picasso's *L'Arlesienne* was significant historically as well as formally, and was informed (as his caption reveals) by Alfred H Barr Jr's retrospective of Picasso's work in 1939.[82] There Barr had identified the painting not only as demonstrative of cubist transparency, simultaneity and intersecting planes, but as Picasso's first double-faced portrait, showing face and profile at the same time, interwoven transparently on the two-dimensional surface. The device of the double-faced portrait was frequently used in Picasso's subsequent works, and was also taken up in photography by Lissitzky and Moholy-Nagy and in graphic design by György Képes.[83] It is with this visual trope in mind that Giedion's cubist interpretation of Lucia Moholy's unusual photograph of the Bauhaus should be read. In his words:

Two major endeavours of modern architecture are fulfilled here, not as unconscious outgrowths of advances in engineering but as the unconscious realisation of an artist's intent; there is the hovering, vertical grouping of planes which satisfies our feeling for a relational space,

ANYTHING BUT LITERAL

and there is the extensive transparency that permits
interior and exterior to be seen simultaneously, en face
and en profile, like Picasso's L'Arlesienne of 1911–12: variety
of levels of reference, or of points of reference, and
simultaneity – the conception of space–time, in short.[84]

Like Picasso's double-faced portrait paintings, what
animates Lucia Moholy's photograph of the Bauhaus is not
the crystalline clarity of the curtain walls but the transparency of the relational space within which the image of the
building remains incomplete and indeterminate. Paradoxically, the multiplication of vantage points in the portraits
displaces the wholeness of physiognomic figuration, and
while promising greater comprehensiveness opens the
domains of identity beyond the physical towards the
non-substantiality of the mental image, which no amount
of multiplication could ever depict with the same objectivity that classical perspective was presumed to have
achieved. These images, then, are more about the relativity
of modern analytics – the technologically mediated
opticality of X-rays, multiple exposures and dissection
(Giedion, like Apollinaire, used the metaphor of surgery to
describe cubism, and by extension engineering)[85] – which
is unable to close the question of knowledge, even as the
light of reason exposed more than had ever been visible
before. In L'Arlesienne, this openness of consciousness to its
own limits is registered especially in the delicate dissolving
of legible features into the illegibility of the formless yet
luminous prismatic field from which they could also be
understood to have magically arisen, like a photographic
image developing in a chemical bath. In this way cubism's
capacity for 'destruction' of form has been turned into
'construction'. Such limits are similarly evident in the
suggestive yet partial view of the Bauhaus complex, in the
dynamic composition of the image focused on the deep
space under the bridge into which the car takes the eye, in
the reciprocal reflection of the bridge in the glazing of the
stair, and in the incomplete glimpse of the interior behind
the curtain wall – its inner mysteries shrouded in darkness

and obscured by radiators, reflections and the interplay of two planes of gridded glass meeting at the corner.

In the end, the transparency that the cubist portrait reveals is paradoxically not of an interior at all but of a luminous yet opaque and misty field, which Giedion called a 'relational space' – an enlarged sphere of perception, neither inside nor outside, within which the image of the figure is tentatively assembled in an open crystalline structure of relationships, as if frozen at a specific moment in the process of its materialisation. 'It suggests', he offered, 'a movement in space that has been seized and held'.[86] Similarly, the open space that is simultaneously between and inside the two wings of the building, that flows freely beyond the frame of the camera and extends into the interior by means of the inward and outward reflection of glass, is at the heart of Giedion's understanding of the Bauhaus. While the camera was able to capture this 'transparent' moment in time and space – this particular intermingling of closed and open, linear architectonics and painterly disintegrations – the subsequent reception of Giedion's book makes clear that the image was unable to transmit graphically to Giedion's readers the unrepresentable experience of space–time that he had hoped it would.

Giedion's history of post-cubist architecture, first published in 1941, was, however, more than a history: it was also a self-fulfilling prophecy by an active protagonist. In the autumn of 1923, in his very first critical writing on contemporary architecture – a review of the Bauhaus exhibition and Bauhaus week – Giedion had already sketched the crucial outlines of this development, not retrospectively but as the programme and potential of modern architecture.[87] The fact that he cited large portions of this text in his book of 1954 on Gropius is a measure of the extent to which Giedion remained committed to his initial vision of what modern architecture might become – a vision that he consistently referred to in relation to cubism.[88] In his 1923 article, he explained that just as all the arts, including architecture and the decorative arts, had for the past decade taken off from painting, so the products of the Bauhaus were to be seen as resting on that foundation as well as on the formal ideals associated with machines. However, he insisted that this had nothing to do with 'a convenient transposition by dexterous opportunists' and could not be the work of a single artist. Instead, he acknowledged the Bauhaus for having drawn together the 'most diligent' masters of abstract painting – Paul Klee, Wassily Kandinsky, Lyonel Feininger and Johannes Itten – for the task of developing the architectural equivalent to the achievements in the other visual arts. The new understanding of the handling of materials as the basis for a new architecture (as it had been the basis for the new painting) was to come 'directly out of the principles of their art', showing that 'cubism is not only a destroyer of form, as people like to say. Rather a new task is assigned to it in the history of art.' Moreover, that task was to continue the shift begun in the seventeenth century when landscape was accepted into painting as a legitimate subject, signalling a shift away from the human-centredness of the Renaissance and towards the non-human,

the increasingly deep, absolute, and precise assumption by all organisms of their own meaning – especially during the empathetic romantic period. The tree, the meadow, and the land become as legible as a human face! Cubism attempts the next step. It attempts to open for us the empire of the inorganic and formless. Its pictures often resemble cellular tissue seen through a microscope. The efforts of the Bauhaus are concerned to eavesdrop on materials and to open up the hidden life of the amorphous. Dead things receive faces and liveliness. The absolute rhythm of things is awoken![89]

Giedion's comments about the Bauhaus – struggling against anthropocentricism while unable to free itself from empathy – came to focus on Kurt Schmidt's *Mechanical Ballet,* performed in Gropius and Meyer's recently completed theatre in Jena. What Giedion admired about the stage set was its attempt at an entirely abstract and hence self-alienating configuration in which people disappeared behind blue, red and yellow planes coming together as 'a cubist picture', set in motion to music.[90] 'Can one sense here', Giedion asked, echoing Behne's post-humanist conception of cubism, 'that things that have nothing to do with humans, animals or trees are opening a new sphere of experience ... always driven back through crystalline fantasy to warmer lands'.[91]

Giedion disregarded the consistently cubic motifs and polychrome interiors of the theatre itself, which Gropius had hoped would be recognised as the architectural fulfilment of Bauhaus ideals, and which van Doesburg had adopted for his conception of architecture. Instead, reiterating a commonplace in architectural discourse, Giedion observed that architecture continued to lag behind the other arts. For Giedion (the engineer turned art historian) it would be in great constructions that the new architecture would take form, allowing new materials – iron, concrete and glass – to speak for themselves in the search for a new feeling for statics. He then pointed to a project exhibited by an unidentified French architect for a concrete house, which reminded him of a crane: buildings with air wafting through them, hovering freely, supported by a single concrete column. 'The means for *Gestaltung*', Giedion observed, 'come once again from cubist fantasy (and give rise to it). Construction is born from the crystal, out of the body, from a sum of crystals, both by the carving out of space as in the baroque.'[92]

With these thoughts Giedion aligned his conception of modern architecture with Oud's programmatic lecture of 1921 and prepared the way for his later 'discovering' in *Bauen in Frankreich* that the potentiality of the industrial structures had been realised in the architecture of Gropius's Bauhaus and Le Corbusier's housing projects, among others. The link between cubism and industrial engineering, so pivotal to his history in *Space, Time, and Architecture*, was already conceptually in place as early as 1923, prior to the demonstration of their union in any examples. By 1928, however, Giedion could cite such a

union for the first time in the domestic architecture of
Le Corbusier, which he compared with the hovering
transparency of his 'cubist' paintings.[93]

Writing *Space, Time, and Architecture* in the late 1930s,
Giedion did not consider either Picasso's *L'Arlesienne* or
Gropius's Bauhaus to represent the pinnacle of artistic
expression in their respective fields; instead he saw them
as having achieved a new clarity of means, which was
subsequently available for more potent symbolic expressions. He cited Picasso's *Guernica* of 1937 as the greatest
contemporary work of art, and distinguished it from the
painter's earlier work as the 'first real historical painting'
of the modern period. Using all the principles and means
of cubism, the painter deployed them here to 'transmute
physical suffering and destruction into powerful symbols'[94]
– symbols that for Giedion played the important role of
mediating between the inner emotional need for harmony
and the turbulent conditions of the external modern
world.[95] Where space–time was characterised by the
interpenetration of inner and outer space, poetic symbols
were understood to mediate between the inner and outer
realms of humanity.

In architecture, Giedion turned to Le Corbusier, first
his housing estate at Pessac (1924–26), then the Villa Savoye
(1928–30) and the League of Nations project (1927),
concluding with a drawing for a steel exhibition structure
for Liège of 1937 juxtaposed with a final example from
Picasso, an almost unrecognisable detail from one of a
series of paintings, each titled *Woman in an Armchair*, of
around 1938.[96] For Giedion, it was only with Le Corbusier
that works of poetic and symbolic value were first attained,
works capable of mediating the division between inner
feeling and outer reason that he considered as endemic to
the transition towards a fully modern age. Recalling once
more Borromini's struggles for the interpenetration of inner
and outer space, and the first attainment of this feeling of
space at the Eiffel tower (which he characterised as a body
without flesh), Giedion focused his enthusiasm for Le
Corbusier on the value of his skeletal Dom-ino system of

concrete construction for achieving the new conception of space–time in the generalisable form of dwellings. As exemplified by the Villa Savoye, 'the body of the house has been hollowed out in every direction: from above and below, within and without. A cross section at any point shows inner and outer space penetrating each other inextricably … as *construction spirituelle'*.[97]

Without recounting Giedion's interpretation of Le Corbusier in detail, what is important here is that Giedion once again pointed to the role of painting in the development of space–time in architecture, reiterating his comparison in *Bauen in Frankreich* between Le Corbusier's *Still Life* of 1924 (signed Jeanneret and displayed in the Pavillon de l'Esprit Nouveau in the following year) and the housing estate at Pessac, and extending this interpretation to the Villa Savoye. Where the early purist paintings by Jeanneret and Amédée Ozenfant (implicitly the point of reference for Rowe and Slutzky's characterisation of purism in terms of clear spatial locations) compressed and layered their purified objects into a two-dimensional spatiality, their subsequent paintings slid out from under the rigour of architectonic objectivism into the fluid, perhaps even oceanic space of humour that Robert Slutzky later de-scribed so eloquently.[98] Their paintings, for which Jeanneret and Ozenfant coined the idea of the *mariage des contours,* internalised the opposition of linear and painterly qualities in a play of perception, illusion and cognition engendered by the simultaneous assertion and denial of volumes. It was this quality that Giedion acknowledged when he wrote that Jeanneret's 'preference for floating, transparent objects whose mass and outlines flow into each other in a *mariage des contours* … leads us from Le Corbusier's pictures to his architecture…'[99] While Rowe and Slutzky took the lan-guage of ambiguity and contradiction from György Képes's 'Language of Vision' (where the marriage of contours was interpreted in terms that echo Giedion's), they used this oscillation and instability nevertheless to support an interpretation of the Villa Stein-de Monzie as an integral and self-referential object. Conjuring a virtual plane of reference immediately behind the garden facade, they likened it to a painting capable of representing the three-dimensional order of the building in two dimensions. In contrast, Giedion followed Le Corbusier's own transposition of his paintings' effects into architecture through colour and the alignment of contours. As Giedion's combination of planar and oblique views suggests, he recognised that Le Corbusier's architecture aimed to dissolve mass into surface for the perception of observers moving in space who were experiencing the phenomenon of parallax: 'corners merging into one another' and clear, independent volumes collapsing into two-dimensionality, to spring back into depth a few steps later.

While Le Corbusier's fascination with perception in motion is well known,[100] what remains less so is the explicitness with which he linked his notion of the architectural promenade to this perceptual play of volumes and colours. In the commentary that accompanies the Villa La Roche-Jeanneret in the *Oeuvre complète*, he described the experience of the promenade not only as a spectacle of perspectives developing with great variety but also as an essay in polychromy that engenders a *camouflage architectural* in which volumes are both 'affirmed and effaced'.[101] This double and contradictory moment – assertion and denial, positive and negative, form and formlessness – was also the key property of the marriage of contours, exploiting the properties of transparent objects (such as bottles) to be at the same time both themselves and not themselves, autonomous and self-estranging, closed and open to the world beyond. Through the techniques of camouflage, the painter-architect attempted to generate the effects of his paintings in architecture.[102]

In the sphere of painting, Jeanneret created an oscillating movement in the eye on an axis with the retina, conforming to a conception of vision as fundamentally two-dimensional and of spatial depth as an effect generated by layered planes. Such a theory had been popularised through Adolf von Hildebrand's treatise of 1893, *The Problem of Form in the Fine Arts*, which privileged the representation of space in classical and neoclassical sculptural reliefs. Later Gestalt psychology also contributed to the diffusion of this theory, which emphasised the totality of the image and relationships of parts to wholes in what amounted to a scientific recasting of classical aesthetics.[103] By basing his theory of vision on the later nineteenth-century optics of psychophysiologists such as Hermann von Helmholtz, Salmon Sticher and Wilhelm Wundt,[104] Hildebrand aimed for the truest representation of objects in space. While the early purist paintings carried similar aspirations, the latter ones dissolved the object into a relational network, a kind of liquid space in which objects and spatial relationships become mutually mediating in perception over time, no longer locked into a binary movement between figure and ground, foreground and background, but now free to move in a less determined way – more lateral, dynamic and open-ended.

Le Corbusier first ventured to transpose this play into architecture by painting the concrete walls of the housing at Pessac in colours that dissolve their mass into surfaces – the same colours as those of his *Still Life* of 1924 – in order to merge the buildings with the landscape. Here and in the later villas, he demonstrated that the medium of architecture differs from painting in that movement takes place in psychophysiological space rather than the purely optical space of the eye. This distinction between two-dimensional and three- or four-dimensional theories of space had already been made in 1919 by Fritz Hoeber in his critique of Hildebrand's aesthetics of space, in which he invoked Schmarsow's theory of the cognition of objects by an observer in motion in order to emphasise that the plastic arts were not configurations merely for the eye but rather for the 'entire organism', the 'experiencing soul'.[105] For Le Corbusier, the experimental projects of van Doesburg and van Eesteren for the De Stijl exhibition of 1923 may well have provided a new way of thinking about the relationship between the spatial effects of two-dimensional painting and the four-dimensional space creation of architecture.[106]

Graham Foundation

Sales Receipt #3624	Store GF
5/2/2019 8:31 PM	Workstation: 1

Graham Foundation Bookshop
4 West Burton Place
Chicago IL 60610
www.grahamfoundation.org
312 787 4071

Cashier

Item Name	Qty.	Price	Ext Price
AA Words 7 Model	1	$22.50	$22.50 T

Disc 10%Event

Subtotal	$22.50
Local Sales Tax @ 10.25% Tax	+ $2.31
RECEIPT TOTAL:	**$24.81**

Debit Card $24.81   XXXXX4542

DEBIT	Expiry Date XX/XX

Reference # 200000029   Auth=083121
Entry: Swiped   Merchant # ***62501

Total Sales Discounts	$2.50

PLEASE RETAIN FOR YOUR RECORDS

Refunds accepted with receipt within 14 days of
purchase

Thank you for visiting the Graham Foundation
Bookshop!

If the transparency of constructions in space–time was, for Giedion, a constituent fact of modern architecture, and clearly he found it in Le Corbusier's work as well as Gropius's, it was not simply a transparency of substance, as Rowe and Slutzky later presumed. Rather it was a transparency of consciousness engendered by works of art and architecture that for him mediated between inner and outer worlds – their status as objects recalibrated to the new technologies of vision as well as industrial production. For Giedion's expanded montage optics, objects were no longer closed (visually and cognitively) but rather had become contingent on the relationships between elements as perceived by observers moving in relation to them over time. The notion of transparency marked the fluid openness with which the new kind of architectural object accorded with the constituent facts of the modern era in which 'no generation is privileged to grasp a work of art from all sides'.[107] That the means of architectonic expression had themselves been rendered transparent (in the sense of a natural language) through rationalisation and purification was a prerequisite for their role as artistic symbols capable of mediating the tragic split between inner feeling and outer rationality,[108] which Giedion considered to be essential for surviving the problematic experiences of modernisation. 'An official art', he explained, has turned its back upon the contemporary world and given up the attempt to interpret it emotionally. The feelings which that world elicits have remained formless, have never met with those objects which are at once their symbols and their satisfaction. Such symbols, however, are vital necessities. Feelings build up within us and form systems; they cannot be discharged through instantaneous animal outcries or grimaces. We need to discover harmonies between our inner states and our surroundings. And no level of development can be maintained if it remains detached from our emotional life. The whole machinery runs down.[109]

Taking into account the history of cubism's reception in German architectural culture, deeply enmeshed in German intellectual traditions and aesthetic theories, Rowe and Slutzky's distinction between literal and phenomenal transparency appears inadequate and forced. Not only was Giedion's understanding of cubism historically valid (at least in part 1) and conceptually provocative, it also aimed to account for the purist architecture of Le Corbusier and to grapple with the ambiguities and indeterminacies of perception and cognition as understood by modern psychology. In Rowe and Slutzky's critique, on the other hand, there was a profound difference between their respective (two- and four-dimensional) interpretations of cubism and their understanding of its potential for architecture. While enjoying the play of *Gestalt* ambiguities characteristic of purist paintings – figure and ground, foreground and background, object and matrix, space and surface – Rowe and Slutzky's game of assertion and denial accepted the experience of doubt, ambiguity and contradiction only by internalising, aestheticising and neutralising its potential to destabilise cognitive certainty. Still committed to an objective aesthetics based on a long outdated theory of optics (Helmholtz), their game was limited to finding ways to represent the spatial structure of the building on the two-dimensional facade for an observer positioned rigidly on axis. Just as Hildebrand privileged relief sculpture for fear that introducing the subject's gaze into the constitution of the object would dissolve its autonomy into the uncontrollable space occupied by the observer,[110] so Rowe and Slutzky sought to secure themselves from the potentially uncontrollable ambiguities and contradictions of the *mariage des contours* – of objects dissolved into an unstable yet constitutive matrix of relationships. While Giedion was likewise motivated by desires for unity, control and consciousness, he nevertheless attempted to rethink the possibility of achieving such conditions through an analysis of the structural conditions of modernity and a recognition that synthetic cubism, collage and montage marked a turn from the determinate representations of a self-positing consciousness towards indeterminate constructions – historical and concrete, yet virtual and ineffable – hovering contingently above the ground.

Originally published in Eve Blau and Nancy Troy (eds.), *Architecture and Cubism* (Cambridge, MA: MIT Press & Canadian Centre for Architecture, 1998), 219–251.

NOTES

1. Colin Rowe and Robert Slutzky, 'Transparency: Literal and Phenomenal', *Perspecta* 8 (1963), 45–54. The essay was first written in 1955–56, and a second part was published in *Perspecta* 13/14 (1971), 287–301.

2. György Képes, *Language of Vision* (Chicago: Paul Theobald, 1944); László Moholy-Nagy, *Vision in Motion* (New York: Wittenborn, 1947).

3. Rowe and Slutzky, 'Transparency', 45–46.

4. Ibid., 48.

5. Manfredo Tafuri and Francesco Dal Co, *Modern Architecture*, trans. Robert Erich Wolf (New York: Harry N Abrams, 1979); see 'Architecture and the Avant-Garde from Cubism to the Bauhaus: 1906–1923', 120–32. Other exceptions include Rosemarie Haag Bletter's critique of Rowe and Slutzky's analysis as 'too erratic to make workable categories' and their 'unorthodox' interpretation of cubism and constructivism as only sensible in formal and not historical terms. See Rosemarie

MODERNITY UNBOUND

Haag Bletter, 'Opaque Transparency', *Oppositions* 13 (Summer 1978), 121–26. In addition, the scholars of the Institut für Geschichte and Theorie der Architektur at the ETH in Zurich have, over the past decade, repeatedly presented and interpreted Giedion's theory of cubism's relation to modern architecture. See Sokratis Georgiadis, *Sigfried Giedion: An Intellectual Biography*, trans. Colin Hall (Edinburgh: Edinburgh University Press, 1993); Dorothee Huber, ed., *Sigfried Giedion. Wege in die Offentlichkeit* (Zurich: Ammann Verlag, 1987); and the exhibition catalogue *Sigfried Giedion 1888–1968. Der Entwurf einer modernen Tradition* (Zurich: Ammann Verlag, 1989). Most recently, Terence Riley has criticised Rowe and Slutzky's conception of transparency while reworking their binary categories to distinguish contemporary projects that employ translucent and reflective surfaces from the transparency ideals of earlier modernist ones. See Terence Riley, 'Light Construction', *in Light Construction* (New York: Museum of Modern Art, 1995), 9–32.

6. The term post-cubist has often been used in relation to purism, a usage that is here expanded to include all the artistic projects and discourses that defined themselves in relation to cubism as either extensions or corrections, including De Stijl, suprematism, the constructivism of El Lissitzky and Czech cubism.

7. See for instance Alfred H Barr Jr, *Cubism and Abstract Art* (New York: Museum of Modern Art, 1936); Walter Curt Behrendt, *Modern Building: Its Nature, Problems, and Forms* (New York: Harcourt, Brace and Company, 1937); and Henry-Russell Hitchcock, *Painting toward Architecture* (New York: Duell, Sloan and Pearce, 1948). Barr's well-known diagram of 'The Development of Abstract Art' charted the lines of influence among the avant-gardes to 1936, and in so doing transformed what had been the programmatic aspirations of post-cubist artists and architects into a statement of historical occurrence.

8. Herwarth Walden, whose gallery, bookstore and magazine *Der Sturm* had been the locus of the avant-garde in Berlin since its founding in 1910, first recognised the Group of Plastic Artists as early as January 1913 in promoting their magazine, *Umelecky mesicnik* (Arts Monthly). By October he had constructed a veritable axis between Prague and Berlin, marked by a group show at his gallery, their participation in his First German Autumn Salon, publication of works by Emil Filla, Karel Čapek, Vincenc Benes and Vlastislav Hofman (the only architect of the group to be featured and its youngest member), and inclusion at the German Werkbund Exhibition in Cologne in July 1914. See Vladimir Slapeta, 'Cubism in Architecture', in Alexander von Vegesack, ed., *Czech Cubism: Architecture, Furniture, and Decorative Arts, 1910–1925* (New York: Princeton Architectural Press, 1992), 34–52; and Georg Bruhl, *Herwarth Walden and 'Der Sturm'* (Cologne: DuMont, 1983).

9. Albert Gleizes and Jean Metzinger, 'Du cubisme' (1912), trans. in Robert L Herbert, ed., *Modern Artists on Art: Ten Unabridged Essays*, trans. T Fisher Unwin and Robert L Herbert (Englewood Cliffs, NJ: Prentice-Hall, 1964), 1–18.

10. Vlastislav Hofman, 'Der Geist der Umwandlung in der bildenden Kunst', *Der Sturm* 5:190–91

(December 1913), 146–147.

11. Bruno Taut, 'Eine Notwendigkeit', *Der Sturm* 4:196–97 (February 1914), 174–75.

12. Adolf Behne, 'Bruno Taut', *Der Sturm* 4:198–99 (February 1914), 182–83.

13. Josef Čapek, 'Moderne Architektur', *Der Sturm* 5:3 (May 1914), 18–19.

14. Adolf Behne, 'Deutsche Expressionisten', *Der Sturm* 5:17–18 (December 1914), 114–15; Adolf Behne, 'Expressionistische Architektur', *Der Sturm* 5:19–20 (January 1915), 135.

15. Heinrich Campendonk, Franz Marc, Oskar Kokoschka, Jacoba van Heemskerck and Carl Mense.

16. Franz Marc, 'Spiritual Treasures' (1912), in Wassily Kandinsky and Franz Marc, eds., *The Blaue Reiter Almanac*, trans. Klaus Lankheit (New York: Da Capo, 1974), 55.

17. Jacob von Uexküll, *Bausteine zu einer biologischen Weltanschauung* (Munich: F Bruckmann, 1913). Behne also cited this book in *Die Wiederkehr der Kunst* (Leipzig: Kurt Wolff, 1919), 109.

18. Adolf Behne, 'Biologie and Kubismus', *Der Sturm* 6:11–12 (September 1915), 71.

19. Implicitly using the notion of artistic *Gestaltung* (form willing or form creation) presented by Konrad Fiedler in the 1880s and popularised by Hermann Konnerth in his book *Die Kunsttheorie Conrad Fiedlers. Eine Darlegung der Gesetzlichkeit der bildenden Kunst* (Munich and Leipzig: R Piper, 1909), Behne considered every work of art a new origin (instinctive expression) and was disdainful of 'cubistic' art that imitated the work of others. Even later he continued to value the work of a 'true' artist over any dogma or canon, often admiring the most disparate-seeming work for its artistic value.

20. Adolf Behne, *Zur neuen Kunst* (Berlin: Sturm, 1914). Behne's book ends by citing Friedrich Nietzsche concerning the value of projecting hopeful images of the future.

21. Adolf Behne, 'Kunstwende?', *Sozialistische Monatshefte* 23–24 (October 1918), 946–52.

22. Behne, 'Biologie und Kubismus', 71.

23. See Herwarth Walden, 'Künstler Volk and Kunst', *Der Sturm* 10:1 (1919–20), 10–11; Nachrevolutionäre', *Der Sturm* 10:3 (1919–20), 36–39; 'Die seidene Schnur,' *Der Sturm* 10:3 (1919–20), 39–45; 'Die Kunst in der Freiheit', *Der Sturm* 10:4 (1919–1920), 50–51; 'Die Freiheit in der Fachkritik', *Der Sturm* 10:4 (1919–20), 51–52.

24. Behne, *Wiederkehr*, 7.

25. Ibid., 14.

26. Ibid., 35, 37.

27. Ibid., 63.

28. Ibid., 38.

29. By calling on artists and architects to bring a new cubist world into being, Behne seized on the sense of immanence that cubism had acquired from its initial reception in Germany following the first exhibition of works by Picasso, Braque, and Derain in September 1910 at the second exhibition of the New Artists' Association in Munich. In his much-read 'Concerning the Spiritual in Art' of the following year, Wassily Kandinsky assigned cubism a founding role not only for modern art but also for the larger 'spiritual revolution' of which he considered it a part. For an introduction to the reception of French cubism in Germany see Peter Selz, *German Expressionist Painting* (Berkeley: University of California Press, 1957), 191–94.

30. For further information on the discourse of new beginnings and its relationship to movements for social reform see Timothy O

Benson, 'Fantasy and Functionality: The Fate of Utopia', in Timothy O Benson, *Expressionist Utopias: Paradise, Metropolis, Architectural Fantasy* (Los Angeles: Los Angeles County Museum of Art, 1994), 12–55.

31. Behne, *Wiederkehr*, 22, 20, 19.

32. Ibid., 24. Kandinsky was no longer included among Behne's list of artists, for he thought that his work remained in the realm of the human.

33. Marcel Franciscono has reported on Gropius's relative ignorance of modern art prior to the war; see Marcel Franciscono, *Walter Gropius and the Creation of the Bauhaus in Weimar: The Ideals and Artistic Theories of Its Founding Years* (Urbana: University of Illinois Press, 1971), 85. It was in Behne's house that Gropius asked Feininger to join him in his new pedagogical venture; see Hans Hess, ed., *Lyonel Feininger* (New York: Abrams, 1961), 87.

34. Behne, *Wiederkehr*, 38, 39.

35. Ibid., 38.

36. Ibid., 66–67.

37. Ibid., 37.

38. Ibid., 64. Behne argued that human beings have capability beyond their desires and knowledge beyond their experience; see 109.

39. Ibid., 59.

40. The 'Exhibition of Unknown Architects' was organised by Gropius with Max Taut and Rudolf Salvisberg for the Workers' Council for Art at IB Neumann's Berlin gallery, Graphisches 1919. Sidestepping existing conceptions of architecture, the show featured the architectonic fantasies of artists next to those of selected architects – utopian fantasies by Hermann Finsterlin, Jefim Golyscheff, Wenzil Hablik, O Herzog, Moritz Melzer, Gerhard Marcks, Arnold Topp, Cesar Klein, Oskar Treichel, Fidus and Johannes Molzahn.

41. Adolf Behne, "'Werkstattbesuche: Jefim Golyscheff,"', *Der Cicerone* II, no. 22 (1919).

42. In *Wiederkehr*, Behne had described the role of art as a godlike creation in an extended philosophical digression that opposed nature to spirit (*Geist*) but argued for an art in which spirit would become nature once again; see 25–36.

43. See Adolf Behne, *Ruf zum Bauen* (Berlin: Wasmuth, 1920), which served as the catalogue for the show 'Neues Bauen' by the Workers' Council for Art. Translated in Charlotte and Tim Benton, eds., *Images* (Milton Keynes: Open University, 1975).

44. See Adolf Behne, 'Architekten', *Frühlicht* I (1921–1922), 55–58; Adolf Behne, 'Neue Kräfte in unser Architektur,' *Feuer* 3 (1921–22), 268–76, rpt. in Haila Ochs, ed., *Adolf Behne, Architekturkritik in der Zeit and Über die Zeit hinaus. Texte 1913–1946* (Basel: Birkhäuser, 1994), 61–67.

45. Adolf Behne, 'Das bunte Magdeburg and die "Miama",' *Seidels Reklame*, October 1922, 201–206, rpt. in Ochs, ed., *Adolf Behne*, 82–92.

46. Letter from Adolf Behne to JJP Oud, 3 October 1920 (Oud Archive, Netherlands Architecture Institute, Rotterdam), cited by Ochs in the foreword to *Adolf Behne*, 11–12.

47. Adolf Behne, 'Neue Kräfte in unserer Architektur', *Feuer* 3 (1921–22), 271, rpt. in Ochs, ed., *Adolf Behne*, 63.

48. See Nancy J Troy, *The De Stijl Environment* (Cambridge, MA: MIT Press, 1983); Alan Doig, *Theo van Doesburg: Painting into Architecture, Theory into Practice* (Cambridge: Cambridge University Press, 1986); Hans Esser, 'JJP Oud,' in Carel Blotkamp et al., *De Stijl: The Formative Years*, trans.

Charlotte Loeb and Arthur L Loeb (Cambridge, MA: MIT Press, 1986), 124–51; and Evert van Straaten, *Theo van Doesburg, Painter and Architect* (The Hague: SDU Publishers, 1988).

49. See Doig, *Theo van Doesburg*, 83–85.

50. See Doig, *Theo van Doesburg*, 33–42, 81, 83–85, 104–105. From his very first considerations of cubism, Oud considered it 'architectonic'; see JJP Oud, 'Over cubisme, futurisme, moderne bouwkunst, enz.,' *Bouwkundig Weekblad* 38:20 (16 September 1916), 156–57. In this article Oud cited Theo van Doesburg, 'De nieuwe beweging in de schilderkunst,' *De Beweging* 12:5–9 (May–September 1916).

51. Jan Gratama, 'Een oordeel over de hedendaagsche bouwkunst in Nederland,' *De Bouwwereld* 21:28 (12 July 1922), 217–19; JJP Oud, 'Bouwkunst en kubisme,' *De Bouwwereld* 21:32 (9 August 1922), 245; Theo van Doesburg, 'Het kubisme voor het laatst,' *De Bouwwereld* 21:35 (30 August 1922), 270. This exchange is reviewed by Doig, *Theo van Doesburg*, 104–105.

52. See Doig, *Theo van Doesburg*, 20–22.

53. See ibid., 21–24.

54. *De Stijl* 9 (1919), 104–105. While unattributed in *De Stijl*, this text was attributed to Behne under the title 'Aufruf' in *Der Cicerone* II (1919), 264.

55. Theo van Doesburg met Gropius together with his partner Adolf Meyer, Fred Forbat and several Bauhaus students in the house of Bruno Taut.

56. See Theo van Doesburg, 'Bilanz des Staatlichen Bauhauses Weimar,' *Mecano*, 1923, back page.

57. Cited by Eberhard Steneberg, *Arbeitsrat für Kunst Berlin 1918–1921* (Dusseldorf: Edition Marzona, 1987), 70.

58. For assessments of van Doesburg's influence see Doig, *Theo van*

Doesburg, 140–41, and Troy, *The De Stijl Environment*, 115–16, 179–84.

59. See Stanford Anderson, *Peter Behrens and the Architecture of Germany 1900–1917* (PhD thesis, Columbia University, 1968), 136–187; and *Masssystem und Raumkunst: das Werk des Architekten, Pädagogen und Raumgestalters JLM Lauweriks* (Krefeld: Kaiser Wilhelm Museum, 1987).

60. HP Berlage, *Grundlagen and Entwicklung der Architektur. Vier Vorträge gehalten im Kunstgewerbemuseum zu Zurich* (Rotterdam: WL and J Brusse, 1908); Adolf Meyer's student project is illustrated and discussed on 56–58. For an account of Meyer's education and his teaching at the Bauhaus, see Annemarie Jaeggi, *Adolf Meyer: Der zweite Mann. Ein Architekt im Schatten von Walter Gropius* (Berlin: Argon, 1994), 20–44, 115–33.

61. Winfried Nerdinger has recounted that the Wasmuth folio on Wright was the 'office bible' and was even consulted by Meyer and Gropius in the design of the Sommerfeld House; see Winfried Nerdinger, *Walter Gropius* (Berlin: Bauhaus Archive, 1985), 54.

62. Oud's interpretation of cubism in architecture remained in currency as late as 1937; see Behrendt, *Modern Building*, 147–50, 152–66.

63. JJP Oud, 'Über die zukünftige Baukunst und ihre architektonischen Möglichkeiten (ein Programm)', *Holländische Architektur* (1926; rpt. Mainz and Berlin: Florian Kupferberg, 1976), 63–76. For an assessment of the relative influence of Oud and van Doesburg for Gropius and Meyer, see Jaeggi, *Adolf Meyer*, 152–69.

64. See Jaeggi, *Adolf Meyer*, 147–52; Esser, 'J J P Oud,' 146–49; and Annemarie Jaeggi, 'Dal blocco

chiuso alla compenetrazione dei volumi,' in *Rassegna* 15, Walter Gropius 1907/1934, 37–46. In this last article, Jaeggi describes the Gropius/Meyer project for the Kallenbach House as their first open composition, in the geometrical rather than functional sense.

65. See Nerdinger, *Walter Gropius*, 54, note 3.

66. This analysis is presented in Yve-Alain Bois, 'The De Stijl Idea,' in *Painting as Model* (Cambridge, MA: MIT Press, 1990), 101–22.

67. See Konrad Fiedler, *On Judging Works of Visual Art* (1876), trans. Henry Schaefer-Simmern and Fulmer Mood (Berkeley: University of California Press, 1949). Fiedler's artistic theories were taken up by Heinrich Wölfflin; see note 19.

68. Theo van Doesburg, *Grundbegriffe der neuen gestaltenden Kunst* (Frankfurt am Main: Oehms, 1925).

69. See Detlef Mertins, 'Playing at Modernity', in *Toys and the Modern Tradition* (Montreal: Canadian Centre for Architecture, 1993), 7–16; and Hanne Bergius, *Das Lachen Dadas. Die Berliner Dadaisten and ihre Aktionen* (Giessen: Anabas, 1993).

70. László Moholy-Nagy, *Von Material zu Architektur* (Munich: Albert Langer, 1928); trans. Daphne M Hoffman and enlarged as *The New Vision* (New York: George Wittenborn, 1947).

71. Giedion's photographs were first published in Sigfried Giedion, 'Zur Situation der französischen Architektur II', *Der Cicerone* 19:6 (1927), 177.

72. Moholy-Nagy, *Von Material zu Architektur*, 236.

73. Walter Gropius, 'glasbau,' *Die Bauzeitung* 23:20 (1926), 159–62, rpt. in Hartmut Probst and Christian Schadlich, eds., *Walter Gropius, Ausgewählte Schriften*, vol. 3 (Berlin:

Ernst & Sohn, 1988), 103–106.

74. Arthur Korn, *Glass in Modern Architecture*, trans. Design Yearbook Limited (London: Barrie & Rockliff, 1967), n.p. This book was reviewed by Ludwig Hilberseimer, together with Konrad Werner Schulze's *Glas in der Architektur der Gegenwart*, in Ludwig Hilberseimer, 'Glas Architektur', *Die Form*, 1929, 521–22; in this article Hilberseimer explicitly linked the emergent glass environment of the late 1920s to Scheerbart's visionary utopia of 1914.

75. Sigfried Giedion, *Space, Time, and Architecture: The Growth of a New Tradition* (Cambridge, MA: Harvard University Press, 1941), 362.

76. Ibid., 14, 404.

77. Ibid., 360.

78. For a detailed consideration of Giedion's conception of space–time in relation to scientific theories, see Sokratis Georgiadis, *Sigfried Giedion*, 97–152; and Sokratis Georgiadis, 'Von der Malerei zur Architektur,' in *Sigfried Giedion: Der Entwurf einer modernen Tradition* (Zurich: Ammann, 1989), 105–17.

79. Giedion's idea of 'space conceptions' plays a similar descriptive and analytical role to Erwin Panofsky's more directly neo-Kantian idea of 'symbolic forms', taken up from Ernst Cassirer. Both Giedion and Panofsky were indebted to Heinrich Wölfflin's categories of epochal visualities and Alois Riegl's notion of a collective *Kunstwollen* that manifests itself in the formal and material structures of works.

80. Giedion refers to construction as the subconscious of the nineteenth century in *Bauen in Frankreich* (Leipzig: Klinkhardt & Biermann, 1928), 2, and in *Space, Time, and Architecture*, where he also refers to the unconscious and automatic writing of the modern age, 162, 207,

583, 584, 586.

81. August Schmarsow, 'The Essence of Architectural Creation' (1893), in Harry Francis Mallgrave and Eleftherios Ikonomou, ed. and trans., *Empathy, Form, and Space: Problems in German Aesthetics 1873–1893* (Santa Monica: Getty Center for the History of Art and the Humanities, 1994), 281–97. While Schmarsow used the idea of *Raumgestaltung* as a space creation that occurs in three dimensions over time, it was also employed by Hildebrand in relation to his two-dimensional theory of space creation.

82. Alfred H Barr Jr, ed., *Picasso: Forty Years of His Art* (New York: Museum of Modern Art, 1939), 77.

83. Képes, *Language of Vision*, was a textbook for modern graphic design based on Gestalt psychology and included numerous examples of double-faced portraits, including his own work and the art of children.

84. Giedion, *Space, Time, and Architecture*, 402.

85. Guillaume Apollinaire, *The Cubist Painters: Aesthetic Mediations* 1913, trans. Lionel Abel (New York: George Wittenborn, 1962), 13, 23. Giedion, *Space, Time, and Architecture*, 358: 'The cubists dissect the object, try to lay hold of its inner composition. They seek to extend the scale of optical vision as contemporary science extends the law of matter. Therefore contemporary spatial approach has to get away from the single point of reference. During the first period (shortly before 1910) this dissection of objects was accomplished, as Alfred Barr expresses it, by breaking up 'the surfaces of the natural forms into angular facets' ... These angles and lines began to grow, to be extended, and suddenly out of them developed one of the constituent facts of space–time representation – the plane.' By later comparing the engineering works of Robert Maillart with Picasso's cubism, Giedion implicitly extended the analysis of cubism to engineering, and reciprocally allowed the constructiveness of engineering to pass to cubism.

86. Giedion, *Space, Time, and Architecture*, 404.

87. Sigfried Giedion, 'Bauhaus und Bauhauswoche zu Weimar', Werk (Zurich), September 1923, rpt. in *Hommage à Giedion. Profile seiner Persönlichkeit* (Basel: Birkhäuser, 1971), 14–19.

88. Sigfried Giedion, *Walter Gropius: Work and Teamwork* (London: Architectural Press, 1954), 31–35.

89. Giedion, 'Bauhaus', 16.

90. The idea that abstraction entailed self-alienation had been advanced in 1908 by Wilhelm Worringer in his well-known *Abstraction and Empathy: A Contribution to the Psychology of Style*, trans. Michael Bullock (New York: International Universities Press, 1953).

91. Giedion, 'Bauhaus', 17.

92. Ibid.

93. For a more extensive treatment of this comparison see also Detlef Mertins, 'Open Contours and Other Autonomies,' in Rodolfo Machado and Rodolphe el-Khoury, eds., *Monolithic Architecture* (New York: Prestel, 1995), 36–61.

94. Giedion, *Space, Time, and Architecture*, 370.

95. For Giedion's theory of the role of artistic symbols, see *Space, Time, and Architecture*, 2–28, and 'Do We Need Artists?', 350–54.

96. Le Corbusier's appreciation of Picasso's art and stature never diminished. The year before Giedion's lectures at Harvard

University, which became *Space, Time, and Architecture*, Walter Curt Behrendt had called Le Corbusier 'the Picasso of modern architecture' who 'uses modern construction mainly for its emotional power of expression'. See Behrendt, *Modern Building*, 161.

97. Giedion, *Space, Time, and Architecture*, 416.

98. Robert Slutzky, 'Aqueous Humor,' *Oppositions* 19/20 (Winter/Spring 1980), 29–51; see also Robert Slutzky, 'Après le Purisme,' *Assemblage* 4 (October 19,97), 95–101, in which he turns to the *mariage des contours* directly as the basis of what he called a new poetic imagination, which he tracks to Le Corbusier's Ronchamp and La Tourette, 'two structures that encapsulate the subliminal and the sublime.' Slutzky writes, 'With Le Corbusier, the constraints of Purist aesthetics, of compositional literalness, will be radically loosened, giving way to more ambiguous space and content and allowing the artist's psychic energies to overflow into his work'.

99. Giedion, *Space, Time, and Architecture*, 408.

100. See for instance Le Corbusier's statement that it is 'by walking, through movement, that one sees an architectural order develop'. Le Corbusier and Pierre Jeanneret, *Oeuvre complète, 1929–1934*, ed. W Boesiger and O Stonorov (Zurich: Editions d'Architecture, 1964), 24.

101. Le Corbusier and Pierre Jeanneret, *Oeuvre complète*, 1910-1929, ed. W Boesiger and O Stonorov (Zurich: Editions d'Architecture, 1964), 60. For discussions of cubism in relation to camouflage see Albert Roskam, 'Dazzle Painting: Art as Camouflage-Camouflage as Art,' *Daidalos* 51 (15 March 1994), 110-15; Roy R Behrens, *Art and Camouflage:*

Concealment and Deception in Nature, Art and War (Cedar Falls: University of Northern Iowa, 1981); and Bruno Reichlin, 'Le Corbusier vs De Stijl,' in Yve-Alain Bois and Bruno Reichlin, eds., *De Stijl et l'architecture en France* (Liège: Pierre Mardaga, 1985), 91–108. Reichlin discusses the relationship between van Doesburg's polychromatic conception of architecture and Le Corbusier's idea of 'architectural camouflage', 105. My interpretation of Le Corbusier's transposition from painting to architecture is also indebted to Yve-Alain Bois' analysis of movement and parallax in the architectural promenade of Le Corbusier at the Villa Savoye; see Yve-Alain Bois, 'A Picturesque Stroll around Clara-Clara,' *October* 29 (1984), 32–62.

102. Jeanneret and Ozenfant had previously disparaged the phenomenon of camouflage in the dazzle-painting of warships using 'cubist' patterns. See Amédée Ozenfant and Charles-Edouard Jeanneret, *Après le cubisme* (Paris: Editions des Commentaires, 1916), 30.

103. Adolf Hildebrand, 'The Problem of Form in the Fine Arts,' trans. in Mallgrave and Ikonomou, eds., *Empathy, Form, and Space*, 227–79. The relationship of Gestalt theory to Hildebrand's treatise, on the one hand, and to modern art, on the other (especially spatial representation in two-dimensional media, including the *mariage des contours*), is evident in Képes's *Language of Vision*, for which Giedion wrote one of the introductory essays.

104. See Mallgrave and Ikonomou, eds., *Empathy, Form, and Space*, 36; and Margaret Iversen, *Alois Riegl: Art History and Theory* (Cambridge, MA: MIT Press, 1993), 73 n.3.

105. Fritz Hoeber, 'Die Irrtümer der Hildebrandschen Raumästhetik', *Der Sturm* 9:12 (March 1919), 157–58. Erwin Panofsky also noted this distinction in *Perspective as Symbolic Form*, trans. Christopher S Wood (New York: Zone Books, 1991), 30.

106. Bruno Reichlin has described Le Corbusier's affinity for van Doesburg's work during the final stage of his Villas La Roche-Jeanneret. See Bruno Reichlin, 'Le Corbusier vs De Stijl', in Bois and Reichlin, eds., *De Stijl et l'architecture en France*, 91–108.

107. Giedion, *Space, Time, and Architecture*, 5.

108. Ibid., 13.

109. Ibid., 351.

110. Yve-Alain Bois has discussed Hildebrand's fear of space – of art leaping from the two-dimensional surface of representation into the three-dimensional world (a fear that he argues Clement Greenberg shared but that Henry-Daniel Kahnweiler and Carl Einstein considered a key limitation of Western art); see Yve-Alain Bois, 'Kahnweiler's Lesson,' in *Painting as Model*, 65–97.

TRANSPARENCY:
AUTONOMY & RELATIONALITY

The binary distinction announced by Colin Rowe and
Robert Slutzky's well-known essay of 1963, 'Transparency:
Literal and Phenomenal', has been deeply absorbed within
American architectural culture.[1] It continues to be
reiterated and reformulated by teachers, critics and even
historians grappling with the shift from orthodox mid-
century modernism to post-modern and post-structural
problematics – grappling all the more now that
contemporary preoccupations have emerged out of, as
much as in reaction to, modernism in its various guises.[2]

Without meaning to detract from the brilliance of Rowe
and Slutzky's essay or to diminish the productive role that
their distinguishing between two 'species' of modernism has
played in architecture, I would like to suggest that this
setting-apart was more complex and unstable than it is
usually taken to have been. Elsewhere I have suggested that
the literal transparency of machine aesthetics – as much
American as German in its conception[3] – is inadequate to the
ideal of transparency promoted by Sigfried Giedion and
László Moholy-Nagy, for which Rowe and Slutzky mobilised the term.[4] As early as 1978, in a largely overlooked
critique, Rosemary Haag Bletter observed that Rowe and
Slutzky's analysis was 'too erratic to make workable
categories', and their 'unorthodox' interpretation of cubism
and constructivism was sensible only in formal and not in
historical terms.[5] Just as Rowe and Slutzky believed that
post-cubist transparency was not as simple as seeing clearly
through glass, so too did Giedion and Moholy-Nagy. Their
concept of transparency was likewise based on a phenomenology of spatial perception, albeit a four-dimensional one
in which the boundaries between inside and outside, subject

and object were dissolved for an observer assumed to be moving freely in space and time. In contrast, Rowe and Slutzky invoked a two-dimensional phenomenology that fixed the observer in a position on axis with the plane of the facade as if viewing a painting. And, while Rowe and Slutzky characterised Giedion as championing Walter Gropius and the Bauhaus at Dessau, in fact Giedion also took the experiments of cubism as the origin of a transparency whose ultimate exemplar in architecture was Le Corbusier's purism.[6] Dividing the avant-garde into two *opposing* camps and favouring one over the other, Rowe and Slutzky staked their distinctive claim to the legacy of cubism, the architecture of Le Corbusier and the phenomenology of space, while dismissing the parallel claims of their opponents and reducing the ambition of their enterprise to something they characterised as simple and 'literal'.

Considered today, however, Rowe and Slutzky's claim should be recognised as based (perhaps unconsciously) on assumptions and *topoi* of the late nineteenth century whose reiteration at the end of the twentieth may be of limited strategic value. Reviewing the formal characteristics that underpinned the categories of literal and phenomenal transparency, one cannot help but be struck by their correspondence to those deployed by Heinrich Wölfflin in forging a distinction between linear and painterly styles, so important for his theory of historical change in art. Wölfflin had inaugurated this influential polarity in *Renaissance and Baroque* of 1888 and later systematised it in his *Principles of Art History* of 1915.[7] While Wölfflin's binary had recast Friedrich Nietzsche's portrayal of the conflict between Apollonian and Dionysian impulses[8] in more psychological, formal and historical terms, Rowe and Slutzky's interpretation of the phenomenal eschewed the issue of historical change and with it the strategic potential of tensions between the formed and the formless. Their preference for the (classical) architectonics of Fernand Léger and Juan Gris displaced the (baroque) movement, disintegration and participation of László Moholy-Nagy and Robert Delaunay as a model for modernism. Instead, they argued for a self-contained form whose underlying theory of spatial and aesthetic perception privileged stasis, flatness and the self-reflexive autonomy of the aesthetic object.[9]

Where Giedion considered modern space to be four-dimensional, indivisible from time and the perception of a subject moving freely in the same space as the object – he called it 'relational space' – Rowe and Slutzky conceived of space as emphatically two-dimensional. For them time, like the viewer, effectively stood still. To be more precise, time was consumed in a movement internal to the eye, for the eye's oscillation between layered planes was thought to generate a thick spatiality. This phenomenal space was considered to be purely optical, in the sense suggested in the late nineteenth century by the aesthetician Konrad Fiedler when he speculated on the possibility of extracting 'pure visibility' as an autonomous element in respect to the object, leaving its tactility behind.[10] The planar model of spatial perception on which Rowe and Slutzky's interpreta-tion rested sought an objective congruence between the physiological optics considered inherent to sight and the self-referentially inscribed form of the building. On this basis, they assumed a new kind of cognition and a new kind of pleasure as the building attempted to present itself in ideal visual terms, faced nevertheless with the limita-tions of material appearances.

Although Rowe and Slutzky's portrait of the garden facade of Le Corbusier's Villa Stein-de-Monzie at Garches (1926–27) is well known, I would like to rehearse it here in order to trace the resonance of its very particular terms with the theory of artistic perception that underlies it. To begin, the authors ask the reader to imagine the villa's facade – they use this classical term, rather than the modernist 'elevation' – as a delaminated version of Fernand Léger's painting *Three Faces* of 1926. They present the building as an analogous 'system of spatial stratification' and 'a field modeled in low relief' in which the impression of depth is generated by fluctuations in figure–ground relations among flat, highly contrasting shapes tied together by horizontal bands and common contours.

In other words, they ask the reader to suspend conventional understanding long enough – or to step back far enough – to consider the cubic volume and internal spatial order of the building as operating exclusively on a two-dimensional surface. As well, they ask the reader to 'enjoy the sensation that *possibly* the framing of the windows passes behind the wall surface', to follow the hint provided by the side walls (set back from the principal plane of the facade) in order to recognise there 'a narrow slot of space traveling parallel to it', and to imagine that, 'bounding this slot of space, and behind it, there lies a plane of which the ground floor, the freestanding walls, and the inner reveals of the doors all form a part'. The authors present this 'imaginary (though scarcely less real) plane that lies behind' as a 'conceptual convenience', instrumental in achieving the cognitive effect of 'our being made conscious of primary concepts which "interpenetrate without optical destruction of each other"'. They draw the reader's eye to other parallel planes, both in front of and behind this slot of space, planes that are incomplete yet contribute to the organisation of the facade in such a way as to imply 'a vertical layerlike stratification of the interior space of the building, a succession of laterally extended spaces traveling one behind the other.'[11]

While the three-dimensionality of the building may not actually be in question, what concerns Rowe and Slutzky is that, from a point deep in the garden and aligned with the central axis of the building, it is possible to entertain an analogy with purist painting and to construct an imaginary model of the entire building in the mind's eye. It was in relation to this capacity of purist architecture to stimulate the imaginative participation of the viewer – configuring a virtual representation of the building which Rosalind Krauss aptly termed a 'hermeneutic phantom' – that Rowe and Slutzky drew on György Képes's Gestalt-based theories of visual communication in *Language of Vision* (1944) in order to set themselves apart from both Giedion and Moholy-Nagy. Yet Képes's book abounds in examples of Moholy-Nagy's work, and Giedion's introduction to it reads like a synopsis of his own *Space,*

Time, and Architecture (1941) – which was after all the central object of Rowe and Slutzky's critique.[12]

Rowe and Slutzky's use of Képes at the expense of his friends and allies was made possible by the way Képes expounded the principles of cubism and post-cubism through the lens of Gestalt theory. Although Moholy-Nagy and Giedion placed considerable emphasis on the role played by cubism in the history of modern art and architecture, Képes's debt to Gestalt theory and its debt in turn to nineteenth-century psychophysiology served to distinguish his interpretation from theirs. Yet Rowe and Slutzky could not have considered Képes's account to be an

'almost classical explanation' of paintings by Georges Braque, Juan Gris and Fernand Léger had it not been foreshadowed within early purism, which presented its linear architectonics as an extension of and a corrective to cubism.

Charles-Edouard Jeanneret
[Le Corbusier], Still Life for
Pavillon de l'Esprit Nouveau, 1924

Although Rowe and Slutzky did not refer to them, the early purist paintings of Jeanneret and Ozenfant were implicitly the point of reference for their characterisation of post-cubism in terms of precise spatial locations. It should be recognised, however, that where these paintings compressed and layered the purified objects that they

Le Corbusier, Quartiers
modernes Frugès, Bordeaux-
Pessac, 1924–27

depicted into a two-dimensional space, subsequent purist paintings slid out from under the rigour of architectonic objectivism into the fluid, perhaps even oceanic, space that Robert Slutzky later described so eloquently.[13] It was these paintings that Giedion (following Jeanneret and Ozenfant) described in terms of the *mariage des contours,* for they internalised the opposition of linear and painterly qualities, in a play of perception, illusion and cognition engendered by the simultaneous assertion and denial of volumes. Where Giedion (once again following Le Corbusier) recognised that achieving the effect of purist paintings in architecture required the manipulation of form and colour for observers moving in psychophysiological space,[14] Rowe and Slutzky, adopting Képes's language of ambiguity, insisted on the primacy of the flat image.[15]

Introducing their notion of 'phenomenal' transparency, Rowe and Slutzky quoted the following passage from *The Language of Vision*, which appears under the heading 'Transparency, interpenetration':

If one sees two or more figures partly overlapping one another, and each of them claims for itself the common overlapped part, then one is confronted with a contradiction of spatial dimensions. To resolve this contradiction, one must assume the presence of a new optical quality. The figures are endowed with transparency; that is, they are able to interpenetrate without an optical destruction of each other. Transparency however implies more than an optical characteristic; it implies a broader spatial order. Transparency means a simultaneous perception of different spatial locations. Space not only recedes but fluctuates in a continuous activity. The position of the transparent figures has equivocal meaning as one sees each figure now as the closer, now as the further one.[16]

What Rowe and Slutzky did not cite, however, were the theories of vision and representation that underlay Képes's argument and the role these played in his polemic, which was aimed at renewing the language of vision. They did not, for instance, note the subject of Képes's book – modern graphic design, not architecture – or the fact that he associated transparency with the *mariage des contours*. Nor did the examples presented by Rowe and Slutzky even approach the diversity of those presented by Képes in support of his argument.[17]

For Képes (echoing Moholy-Nagy and Giedion as well

as Ozenfant and Jeanneret) modern vision needed to be resynchronised to the conditions of modern technology, which had, he suggested, finally succeeded in breaking down the old system of perspectival representation. He believed that new technologies of photography and film had opened up an opportunity to renew a mode of visual representation that was more congruent with what he took to be the biological conditions of human perception – a form of representation on a flat surface, similar to non-Western and pre-perspectival painting, as well as the naive drawings made by children.

Képes's opening section on 'plastic organisation' laid the theoretical foundation (interpolated from Gestalt theory[18]) for his claim that these other forms of representation – at once more primitive and more modern – were also more natural. He suggested that, like the anatomist, the perspectivalist achieved knowledge as well as the optical and scientific mastery of nature only at the expense of the living, moving aspects of the body, 'the flux of the innumerable visual relationships that the visible world has for the spectator'. For Képes, perspective 'froze the living, fluctuating wealth of the visual field into a static geometrical system, eliminating the time-element always present in the experiencing of space, and thus destroying the dynamic relationships in the experience of the spectator.'[19]

Within Képes's two-dimensional post-perspectival theory of spatial representation, images played a number of interrelated roles. They mediated between the inner and the outer world, not in the fixed, unequivocal and absolute manner of perspective, but rather in engaging the viewer's participation. This, he thought, occurred in several ways. Because both the eye and the picture plane have a limited ability to register depth and space, Képes held that the viewer's perceptual apparatus was constantly engaged in resolving contradictory information.[20] He believed that such material deficiencies required that the observer take an active role in forming the object, or at least its virtual *Gestalt*. 'Every experiencing', Képes wrote, 'is a forming; a dynamic process of integration, a "plastic" experience'.[21]

Equivocal images such as overlapping planes or the
'marriage of contours' provide opportunities for the
spectator to engage in the natural process of integrating
space with knowledge of the objects depicted at the level
of apperception or habit. Képes argued that visual images
should achieve this kind of dynamic interaction between
tension and balance,[22] attraction and repulsion,[23] figure
and ground, creating 'not a facade but a living, flowing
space' – a space–time that offers opportunities for 'wider
and deeper human experiences'.[24] Such images were
thought to transform the two-dimensionality of the surface
into a spatialised field that nevertheless retained its
two-dimensionality even as it integrated the third and
fourth dimensions.

Rowe and Slutzky's reading of Képes's treatise was
selective in ways that side-stepped his preoccupation with
living, flowing space – even in two-dimensional graphic
design – which they associated with the 'literal' machinist
and constructivist 'species' of modernism. While not
immune to the claims of Gestalt to be an absolute perceptual science or to Képes's aspiration to modernise vision
in objective terms, they focused instead on his notion that
contradiction, ambiguity and tension in visual representation – the oscillation of figure and ground, near and far,
inside and outside generated by overlapping planes –
were essential to achieving a balanced ecology of human
perception. For Rowe and Slutzky such contradictions
were a source of aesthetic pleasure: the pleasures of space
released in the tension of perception that weaves discon-
nected elements into a unified yet ambiguous and unstable
two-dimensional image.

As Képes acknowledged, the roots of Gestalt theories
of perception and psychology lie in the late nineteenth-
century psychophysiological research of figures such as
Wilhelm Wundt, Hermann von Helmholtz and Theodor
Lipps. These theorists had already combined science and
philosophy into several kinds of 'scientific aesthetics',
which in turn had served artists seeking to reground their
practice on a supposedly objective basis as a response to the

critique of imitation, naturalism and perspective. In this respect, Képes's book belongs to a series of theoretical-historical treatises written by artists and informed by art historians and aestheticians – a series that would include writings by August Endell, Wassily Kandinsky, Johannes Itten, Paul Klee, László Moholy-Nagy, as well as Ozenfant and Le Corbusier. It is nevertheless curious to find the optical theories of Helmholtz so explicitly foregrounded in Képes's book, some 60 years after they were first formulated and long after their scientific authority had been eclipsed. Képes cited Helmholtz directly, not only in setting out his understanding of spatial perception as a function of muscular movements in the eye (compensating for inherent limitations such as the two-dimensionality of the retinal image[25]), but also in discussing colour theory and after-images,[26] the origins of linear perspective,[27] and the importance, for physiological optics, of studying the paintings of great masters.[28]

In his own time Helmholtz's theory of artistic vision as fundamentally two-dimensional had been of great consequence to the sculptor and theorist Adolf Hildebrand, who together with Konrad Fiedler and the painter Hans von Marées was part of a well-known and influential trio of formalists.[29] In his much-read treatise of 1893, *The Problem of Form in the Fine Arts*,[30] Hildebrand explained that the aim of art was to bring nature into relation with the visual faculties,[31] which he understood as fundamentally two-dimensional, following the theories of vision by Helmholtz (whose work he read and whose bust he sculpted), Salmon Sticher and Wilhelm Wundt.[32] While he acknowledged the importance of stereoscopic vision for life in three dimensions, he favoured two-dimensional monocular vision for art. 'The painter', he wrote, 'gives on a plane a visual impression of a three-dimensional form, while the sculptor forms something three-dimensional for the purpose of affording a plane visual impression.'[33] Only in this way could what he called 'effective form', as distinct from 'inherent form', be created, and a clear comprehension of the values of spatial form as such be achieved.[34] These catego-

ries may be understood as one of the *topoi* below the surface
of Rowe and Slutzky's later distinction between phenomenal and literal transparency. For Hildebrand, the problem
of form in relief focused on how the different planes of the
image, representing different objects at different distances,
work together within an effective system. Such a system
presents objects as coherent surface images, their spatial
form evoked by means of an attraction of the eye into
depth. Movement into depth was also thought to require
a background, a surface against which the figure stands
out coherently. The double demand for unified surface
image and movement into depth was to be resolved by the
technique of superimposition, which conceals at the same
time as it connects, thereby enhancing surface unity
without sacrificing the distinctions of distance.[35]

Not surprisingly, Hildebrand privileged relief
sculpture, especially that of ancient Greece, which he
declared to be paradigmatic for the presentation of three-
dimensional impressions. His own sculptures as well as the
paintings of von Marées, with their overlapping compositional structures and relief built up with pigment, demonstrated how the effect of spatial depth could be achieved
while maintaining the integrity of the two-dimensional
surface.[36] In introducing the concept of relief, Hildebrand
reiterated his proposition that with 'an ever more concentrated juxtaposition of objective surface effects' the sculptor
was able to achieve 'a simple idea of volume, that is, of a
surface that extends into depth'.[37] To illustrate this principle
he drew the following analogy, which bears a striking
correspondence to Rowe and Slutzky's imaginary slot of
space at the Villa Stein – so striking as to render explicit
the theoretical assumptions implicit in the critics' reading:

**Imagine a figure placed between two parallel planes of
glass, positioned in such a way that the figure's outermost
points touch the glass. The figure then occupies and
describes a space of uniform depth, within which its
component parts are arranged. Seen from the front
through the glass, the figure is coherent, first as an**

identifiable object within a uniform planar stratum, second as a volume defined by the uniform depth of the general volume. The figure lives, so to speak, in a *planar stratum of uniform* depth, and each form tends to spread out along the surface, that is, to make itself recognizable. Its outermost parts, touching the panes, continue to lie on a single plane, even if the panes are taken away.[38]

For Hildebrand the true artistic object was 'a planar stratum of uniform depth' and the total volume of the picture was produced by 'a number of such imaginary strata placed one behind another in a series'. The distinctive achievement of an artist working in this way was to create an image of space and form which in actuality was a compound of countless kinaesthetic images in which 'what remains is a surface impression that strongly suggests the idea of depth: one that the calmly observing eye is able to take in without any kinaesthetic activity'.[39] 'Visual perception', Hildebrand believed, occurred when the eye at rest took in a 'distant view', as it was inclined to do, while 'kinaesthetic perception' was concerned with the 'near view', in which the eye engaged in a series of movements in order to grasp the object as a whole. To perceive spatial depth, he believed, there was a need for a particular type of movement in the eye that would coordinate the two modes of vision in an 'effective form' which conformed to the truth of perception. The idea of truth to nature was of no consequence to Hildebrand, for whom the purpose of art was to create a distinct and autonomous world of perception – a world constituted specifically for the aesthetic pleasure of humanity.

Yve-Alain Bois has suggested that a profound fear of space motivated this insistence by Hildebrand on the autonomy of the domain of art, a 'fear of seeing the sculptural object lose itself in the world of objects, fear of seeing the limits of art blur as real space invaded the imaginary space of art'.[40] The sculptor had condemned the nineteenth-century panorama, the figures in waxworks and the tombs of Canova, all of which played with the ambiguous boundaries between 'real' space and 'representational' space. According to Bois, Hildebrand's conception of sculpture as painting, reiterated in the post-war period by the American formalist critic Clement Greenberg in his interpretation of Picasso's cubist constructions and David Smith's sculptures,[41] aimed, like Rowe and Slutzky's conception of architecture as painting, at safeguarding art from the terrifying prospect of the dissolution of the distinction between the autonomous space of the art object and real space. This fear had been absorbed within bourgeois art in the nineteenth century, which was withdrawing from the destabilising experience of industrialisation, modernisation and metropolitanisation into the autonomous self-referential interior of artistic forms and practices – knowable, controllable and secure.[42] Like Greenberg, the critic Michael Fried was fearful of the emergence of a relational conception of art, the greatest threat of which he identified in minimalism, or what he called 'literalist' art.[43] Robert Somol has already commented on the correspondence of terms and critiques between Rowe and Fried, and has even pointed to a possible way of revaluing the category of the 'literal' in architecture through the notion of repetition.[44] Here, however, I would like to expand this to suggest that the relationality of the 'literal' prefigures certain aspects of contemporary theory. Just as Rosalind Krauss began her reading of minimalist art by revaluing what Fried feared about it – recognising its 'theatricality', or its being in the space and time of the observer, as the basis of its strategic contribution to the history of post-formalism and the early history of post-modernism – so I would like to point to Giedion and Moholy-Nagy for their pre-minimalist (although still idealist) conception of relational space, which was likewise opposed to formalist autonomy and was already engaged in the concrete historical conditions of the space occupied by both the work of art and the observer.[45]

The aesthetic effect that interested Rowe and Slutzky was not the dissolution of substance into the particles of space, which had underpinned Alois Riegl's 'impressionist' reading of late Roman art works, or the flowing *Raumgestal-tung* of Moholy-Nagy's constructivism, or the formlessness of van Doesburg's quest for a 'cubist' four-dimensional architecture. Rather, they sought the hermeneutic pleasure of an almost complete self-referentiality – one that absorbed doubt without compromising cognitive efficacy. Enjoying the play of Gestalt ambiguities that was characteristic of purist paintings – figure and ground, object and matrix, space and surface – Rowe and Slutzky's game of assertion and denial accepted the experience of doubt, ambiguity and contradiction, which accompanied the emergence of subjective aesthetics, only by internalising, aestheticising, and neutralising its potential to destabilise cognitive certainty. Based still on an objectivist aesthetics of subjective reception (Hildebrand), itself based on an outdated objectivist optics (Helmholtz), their appreciation of purist still-lifes and Le Corbusier's Villa Stein limited the game to the frame of the two-dimensional plane, charged with the obligation of representing the spatial structure of the building for an observer aligned perspectively on axis.

Just as Hildebrand privileged relief sculpture out of a fear that introducing the subject's gaze into the constitution of the art object would dissolve its autonomy into the uncontrollable space occupied by the observer,[46] so Rowe and Slutzky pulled back from the implications for architecture of the potentially uncontrollable ambiguities and contradictions of the *mariage des contours* – of the object dissolved into a liquid field of unstable yet constitutive relationships. They reasserted the pictorial facade as the guarantor of self-reflexive transparency. Notwithstanding her admiration for the formalist tradition with which she associated Rowe, it was this approach that prompted Krauss, in her essay of 1980, to reject formalism in favour of structuralism. She argued that the formalists' demand for 'examining the ground of its own access to knowledge' – which earlier she had valued for turning transparency into opacity – simply resulted in a second-order transparency, still grounded in the proposition of an intelligence that is transparent to itself.

While Giedion was likewise motivated by the desire for unity, control and consciousness, he nevertheless attempted to rethink the possibility of achieving such conditions through an analysis of the structural and material conditions of modernity. He recognised that synthetic cubism, collage and montage marked a turn from the determinate representation of a self-positing consciousness towards a 'new optics' of indeterminate biotechnic constructions hovering contingently without ground in a relational space that is as historical and concrete as it is virtual and ineffable. Beyond the label of literal, the ideal of transparency that Giedion and Moholy-Nagy sought to articulate in the 1920s, 1930s and 1940s was phenomenal and perceptual, after all, in its confrontation with the machine, or more precisely with modes of production and reception in the modern industrial era. As such, it may yet figure in our understanding of the prehistory of contemporary preoccupations with systems of mediation, on the one hand, and the immediacy of formlessness on the other.

Originally published in *AA Files* 32 (1997), 3–11.

MODERNITY UNBOUND

NOTES

1. Colin Rowe and Robert Slutzky, 'Transparency: Literal and Phenomenal', *Perspecta* 8 (1963), 45–54. The extent to which Gestalt psychology informed this essay is more explicit in its sequel, 'Transparency: Literal and Phenomenal, Part II', *Perspecta* 13/14 (1971), 287–301.

2. The most considered critical treatments of the distinction between literal and phenomenal transparency are by Rosalind Krauss, 'Death of a Hermeneutic Phantom', *Architecture + Urbanism* 112 (January 1980), 189–219; Anthony Vidler, 'Transparency', *The Architectural Uncanny* (Cambridge, MA: MIT Press, 1992), 218–19; Terence Riley, *Light Construction* (New York: Museum of Modern Art, 1995); and Robert Somol, 'Oublier Rowe', *Formwork: Colin Rowe, ANY 7/8* (1994), 8–15. These critics have understood the issue of transparency in cognitive as well as visual terms – of the modern subject believing that ideas, forms and interpretations can be transparent to the mind that thinks them.

3. See for instance Alfred H Barr Jr's influential exhibition Machine Art of 1934 at the Museum of Modern Art. Exhibition catalogue: *Machine Art* (New York: MoMA, 1934).

4. See Detlef Mertins, 'Anything But Literal: Sigfried Giedion and the Reception of Cubism in Germany', in *Architecture and Cubism*, eds. Nancy Troy and Eve Blau (Cambridge, MA: MIT Press, 1997). See also D Mertins, 'System and Freedom: Sigfried Giedion, Emil Kaufmann and the Constitution of Architectural Modernity', in *The Origins of the Avant-Garde in America, 1923–1949*, ed. Robert Somol (New York, Monacelli Press, 1996).

5. See Rosemary Haag Bletter, 'Opaque Transparency', *Oppositions* 13 (Summer 1978), 121–6.

6. See Sigfried Giedion, *Space, Time, and Architecture* (Cambridge, MA: Harvard University Press, 1941).

7. See Heinrich Wölfflin, *Renaissance und Barock. Eine Untersuchung über Wesen und Entstehung des Barockstils in Italien* (Munich: Theodor Ackermann, 1988), partially translated by Kathrin Simon as *Renaissance and Baroque* (Ithaca, NY: Cornell University Press, 1964). See also H Wölfflin, *Kunstgeschichtliche Grundbegriffe. Das Problem der Stilentwicklung in der neueren Kunst* (Munich: Hugo Bruckmann, 1915), trans. by MD Hottinger as *Principles of Art History: The Problem of the Development of Style in Later Art* (New York: Dover, 1950). For the sources of Wölfflin's categories and the significance of Jacob Burckhardt, who also taught Nietzsche, see Joan Goldhammer Hart, 'Heinrich Wölfflin: An Intellectual Biography' (unpublished dissertation, University of California, Berkeley, 1981), 139–211. For an interpretation of Wölfflin's categories in relation to Nietzsche's Apollonian and Dionysian, see Jan Bailostocki, '"Barok": Stil, Epoche, Haltung', in *Stil und Ikonographie* (Dresden, 1965), 80.

8. Friedrich Nietzsche, 'The Birth of Tragedy: Out of the Spirit of Music', in *The Birth of Tragedy and the Case of Wagner*, translated by Walter Kaufmann (New York: Vintage Books, 1967).

9. For a post-structural analysis of Rowe's thought in relation to issues of autonomy and form, see RE Somol, 'Oublier Rowe', *Formwork: Colin Rowe*.

10. See Konrad Fiedler, 'Über dem Ursprung der künstlerischen

Tätigkeit' (1887), in K Fiedler, *Schriften zur Kunst*, vol. I, edited by Gottfried Boehm (Munich: Wilhelm Fink, 1971), 183–367. While Giedion also emphasised vision (the 'new optics'), it was the embodied vision of an observer moving in space and time that he had in mind, just as he often used corporeal metaphors to characterise buildings.

11. Rowe and Slutzky, 'Transparency', 49.

12. György Képes, *Language of Vision* (Chicago: Paul Theobald and Company, 1944). Képes was much younger than Moholy-Nagy and settled in Berlin in 1931 under the latter's influence. He then followed Moholy-Nagy to London, where they worked together, and later to Chicago, where Képes taught in Moholy-Nagy's New Bauhaus. See Krisztina Passuth, *Moholy-Nagy* (London: Thames & Hudson, 1985), 60, 65, 69, 70. If Képes initially drew on Moholy-Nagy and Giedion, Giedion's later thought on transparency in primitive as well as modern art bears traces of Képes's *Language of Vision*. See S Giedion, 'Transparency: Primitive and Modern', *Art News*, 51:4 (June–August 1952), 47–50, 92–6.

13. Robert Slutzky, 'Aqueous Humor', *Oppositions* 19/20, Winter/Spring 1980, 29–51; see also R Slutzky, 'Après le Purisme', *Assemblage* 4, October 1987, 95–101, in which he turns to the *mariage des contours* as the basis of what he called a new poetic imagination, which he tracks to Le Corbusier's Ronchamp and La Tourette, 'two structures that encapsulate the subliminal and the sublime'. Slutzky writes, 'With Le Corbusier, the constraints of Purist aesthetics, of compositional literalness, will be radically loosened, giving way to more ambiguous space and content and allowing the artist's psychic energies to overflow into his work'.

14. For a detailed reconsideration of Giedion's interpretation of the relationship between Le Corbusier's architecture and his purist paintings, see D Mertins, 'Anything But Literal', in *Architecture and Cubism*. An earlier version of this was published in D Mertins, 'Open Contours and Other Autonomies', *Monolithic Architecture*, eds. Rodolfo Machado and Rodolphe el-Khoury (New York: Prestel, 1996), 36–61.

15. Le Corbusier's fascination with perception in motion is well known. What remains less well known, however, is the explicitness with which he linked his notion of the architectural promenade to the perceptual play of volumes and colours. See D Mertins, 'Anything But Literal'.

Underlying Giedion and Moholy-Nagy's concern for the moving spectator was the theory of *Raumgestaltung* (space-forming) developed by the art historian August Schmarsow. See Schmarsow, 'The Essence of Architectural Creation' (1893), in *Empathy, Form, and Space*, edited and translated by Harry Francis Mallgrave and Eleftherios Ikonomou (Santa Monica: Getty Center for the History of Art and the Humanities, 1994), 281–97; and Mitchell Schwarzer, 'The Emergence of Architectural Space: August Schmarsow's Theory of *Raumgestaltung*', *Assemblage* 15 (1991), 50–61.

In 1919, Fritz Hoeber invoked Schmarsow's theory of the cognition of objects by an observer in motion in a critique of Hildebrand, in order to emphasise that the plastic arts were not configurations merely for the eye, but rather for the 'entire

organism', the 'experiencing soul'.
See Fritz Hoeber, 'Die Irrtümer der
Hildebrandschen Raumästhetik',
Der Sturm, 9:12 (March 1919), 157–58.

16. Képes, *Language*, 77.

17. Ibid., 76–85. Képes grouped
together, for instance, a study
of transparency by his student
Clifford Eitel, a fifteenth-century
German painting of the Last Supper
in association with a diagram of
overlapping planes, Picasso's
portrait of Kahnweiler, a still life by
Ozenfant, a photograph of a layered
view through a house by GF Keck,
a space construction of 1930 by
Moholy-Nagy, a photomontage made
by Képes himself and one by Jack
Waldheim, a double portrait drawing
by Le Corbusier and numerous
examples of advertising including
images by Képes, William Burtin,
Paul Rand, Frank Barr, Cassandre, E
McKnight Kauffer and Fernand Léger.

18. Képes begins his acknowlegements
in *Language of Vision* with the
following statement: 'First of all
the author wishes to acknowledge
his indebtedness to the Gestalt
psychologists. Many of the inspiring
ideas and concrete illustrations
of Max Wertheimer, K Koffka and
W Kohler, have been used in the
first part of the book to explain the
laws of visual organisation.' Képes,
Language, 4.

19. Képes, *Language*, 86.

20. Ibid., 68.

21. Ibid., 15.

22. Ibid., 35.

23. Ibid., 32, 60.

24. Ibid., 66.

25. Ibid., 34, 171.

26. Ibid., 35.

27. Ibid., 86.

28. Ibid., 161.

29. See *Hans von Marées*, edited by
Christian Lenz (Munich: Prestel,
1987), and Alfred Neumeyer, 'Hans

von Marées and the Classical
Doctrine in the Nineteenth
Century', *Art Bulletin* (1938), vol.
20, 291–311. Von Marées' paintings
were included in Paul Fechter's
Expressionismus (1914) along with
cubist paintings by Picasso and
Braque, and later in Paul Küpper's
Kubismus (1921). This was a sign not
only of the extent to which the
German discourse of expressionism
sought to absorb the whole of
modern painting but also of the fluid
reciprocity between expressionism
and cubism in the German scene at
that time. Julius Meirer-Graefe, in
Hans von Marées (Munich: R Piper &
Co., 1920), celebrated von Marées as
the equal of Paul Cézanne.

30. Adolf Hildebrand, 'The Problem
of Form in the Fine Arts, 1893', in
Empathy, Form, and Space, 227–79.
For a discussion of the relationship
of Alois Riegl's thought to that of
Hildebrand, see Margaret Iversen,
Alois Riegl: Art History and Theory
(Cambridge, MA: MIT Press, 1991),
73–76.

31. Hildebrand, 'Problem of Form', 232.

32. See 'Introduction', *Empathy, Form,
and Space*, 36, and Iversen, *Alois
Riegl*, 73, footnote 3.

33. Hildebrand, 'Problem of Form', 232.

34. Ibid., 236.

35. Ibid., 247.

36. On Hildebrand's technique,
see Helmut Börsch-Supan, 'Zur
Herkunft der Kunst von Marées', in
Hans von Marées, 25–32.

37. Hildebrand, 'Problem of Form,' 251.

38. Ibid.

39. Ibid., 252.

40. Ibid., 75.

41. See Clement Greenberg, 'Review of
the Exhibition Collage' (1948; rpt.
*Clement Greenberg: The Collected
Essays and Criticism*, vol. 2, ed.
John O'Brian (Chicago: University
of Chicago Press, 1986), 259–63, and

C Greenberg, 'The New Sculpture' (1949; rpt. in O'Brian). For a more detailed reading of these issues in relation to Greenberg, Fried and Krauss, see D Mertins in *Monolithic Architecture*.

42. For the relationship between autonomous art and avant-garde art, see Peter Bürger, *Theory of the Avant-Garde*, trans. Michael Shaw (Minneapolis: University of Minnesota, 1984), and the foreword by Jochen Schulte-Sasse, 'Theory of Modernism versus Theory of the Avant-Garde', vii–xlvii. It was against this fear among the bourgeoisie that the avant-gardes, especially the dadaist–constructivist axis in Germany, mounted their campaign after the war, to re-engage art in social praxis, moving from painting to architecture.

43. Michael Fried, 'Art and Objecthood' (1967; rpt. in *Minimal Art: A Critical Anthology*, edited by Gregory Battcock (New York: EP Dutton, 1968), 116–47.

44. See RE Somol, 'Oublier Rowe', *Formwork: Colin Rowe*, 15.

45. See Rosalind Krauss, *Passages in Modern Sculpture* (Cambridge, MA: MIT Press, 1977), 201–42. Of course the distinction Krauss made in this text between the theatricality of Moholy-Nagy's Light *Space Modulator* of 1923–30 and that of Picabia's stage set for Relâche of 1924 is still significant. See also R Krauss, 'Sculpture in the Expanded Field', *October* 8 (Spring 1979), and R Krauss, 'Overcoming the Limits of Matter: On Revising Minimalism', in *American Art of the 1960s*, ed. John Elderfield (New York: Museum of Modern Art, 1991), 123–41 (especially 138–39).

For an interpretation of space-time in the relational aesthetics of art during the 1990s, see Nicholas Bourriaud, 'An Introduction to Relational Aesthetics', in Traffic, exhibition catalogue (Bordeaux: Cap Musée d'Art Contemporain, 1966), unpaginated.

46. Yve-Alain Bois has discussed Hildebrand's fear of space – of art leaping from the two-dimensional surface of representation into the three-dimensional world (a fear, he argues, that Clement Greenberg shared but that Henry-Daniel Kahnweiler and Carl Einstein considered a key limitation of Western art). See Bois, 'Kahnweiler's Lesson', in *Painting as Model* (Cambridge, MA: MIT Press, 1990), 65–97.

THE ENTICING AND THREATENING
FACE OF PREHISTORY:
WALTER BENJAMIN AND THE UTOPIA
OF GLASS

CONCRETE

Consider a detail, or actually several related details from
Walter Benjamin's reading of modern architecture and its
historical origins in the iron and glass constructions of
nineteenth-century Parisian arcades, exhibition halls and
department stores. Not only was Benjamin so 'electrified'
by his first glimpse into Sigfried Giedion's 1928 *Building
in France, Building in Iron, Building in Concrete* that he
immediately put it down again until he 'was more in touch
with my own investigations' – referring in all probability
to his well-known *Arcades Project* – but when he returned
to Giedion's book shortly thereafter, he began reading it
backwards. Furthermore, the last section, depicting the
architectural history of reinforced concrete, so impressed
him that before turning to the rest of the book, which
concerned iron construction, he wrote Giedion an
immensely complimentary letter and suggested that they
might meet in Paris during the spring.[1] Given the strategic
importance of iron for Benjamin's prehistory of modernity,
this enthusiasm for concrete is quite surprising, as is his
apparent lack of interest in Giedion's genealogy of iron
morphologies.

But consider a further detail. Four months after
writing his letter to Giedion, Benjamin published a short
text describing his admiration for several 'books that
have remained alive', including Alfred Gotthold Meyer's
Eisenbauten (Iron Constructions) of 1907.[2] While

acknowledging Giedion's book within his tribute to Meyer, Benjamin gave pride of place to the earlier study, which predated the major developments in concrete but attended confidently to the role of construction in bringing into existence new conditions for building, dwelling and spatial experience. For Benjamin,

This book continues to astonish us thanks to the farsight-edness with which the laws of technical construction, which through the dwelling become the laws of life itself, were recognised and identified with uncompromising clarity at the beginning of the century... But what makes Meyer's book so exceptional is the assurance with which it succeeds again and again in situating the iron construc-tion of the nineteenth century within the context of the history and prehistory of building, of the house itself. [Meyer's and Giedion's books] are prolegomena to any future historical materialist history of architecture.[3]

Where Meyer had recognised that the future of iron would be bound up with reinforced concrete, it remained for Giedion to tell the story of how this new kind of 'stone' developed technically and how the great architect-con-structors Auguste Perret, Tony Garnier and Le Corbusier turned it into the privileged medium for materialising new forms of life during the first decades of the twentieth century. According to Giedion, where the earlier generation had successfully addressed the importance of utilitarian buildings, it was the task of the current generation, among whom he recognised Le Corbusier as leader, 'to take the problem of dwelling from individual dilettantism and pseudo-handicraft production into the realm of industrial standardisation through the most precise comprehension of living functions'. Beginning with the proposition that the house must be thoroughly bathed in air, Giedion portrays Le Corbusier's distinctive achievement as having reinter-preted spare concrete construction into a new form of dwelling, an 'eternally open house' – his concrete 'Dom-ino' skeleton – whose generalisable applicability he had demonstrated in his housing estate in Pessac-Bordeaux, France, of 1924–27. Giedion presents Le Corbusier's housing project, as the architect himself did, as following from Tony Garnier's dramatic utopian vision for a new kind of city – his light, loose and limber 'Cité industrielle' of 1904. In the 'fantastic expansion' that grows out of the cellular arrangements of cubic houses in garden settings, Giedion 'feels the connection between rationality and vision which the emerging age delineates perhaps most sharply'.[4]

Coming to the defence of the Pessac housing, often accused of being 'as thin as paper,' Giedion explains that 'the solid volume is eaten away wherever possible with cubes of air and rows of windows suddenly passing into the sky'. Elaborating on the revolutionary implications, he writes

Corbusier's houses are neither spatial nor plastic: air flows through them! Air becomes a constituent factor! Neither space nor plastic form counts, only RELATION and INTERPENETRATION! There is only a single, indivisible space. The shells fall away between interior and exterior. Yes, Corbusier's houses seem thin as paper. They remind us, if you will, of the fragile wall paintings of Pompeii. What they express in reality, however, coincides completely with the will expressed in all of abstract painting. We should not compare them to paper and to Pompeii but point to Cubist paintings, in which things are seen in a floating transparency, and to the Purist [Charles-Edouard] Jeanneret himself, who as architect has assumed the name Le Corbusier. In his *Peinture moderne* … he likes to assure us that he has deliberately chosen only the most ordinary bottles and glasses, that is, the most uninteresting objects, for his pictures so as not to detract attention from the painting. But the historian does not see this choice as accidental. For him the significance of this choice lies in the preference for floating, transparent objects whose contours flow weightlessly into each other. He points from the pictures to the architecture. Not only in photos but also in reality do the edges of houses blur.

There arises – as with certain lighting conditions in snowy
landscapes – that dematerialization of solid demarcation
that distinguishes neither rise nor fall and that gradually
produces the feeling of walking in clouds.[5]

It was enthusiastic prose such as this, about the new
abstractly technological domestic architecture – hovering
open cubes of air capable of engendering in architecture the
effect of paintings in which transparent interpenetrating
glass objects generate an unprecedented kind of spatial
liquidity – that so 'electrified' Benjamin at a time when he
was preparing his essay on surrealism, published just two
weeks before his letter to Giedion.[6] And it was in this essay
that he first invoked the houses of Le Corbusier, along with
those of the Dutch functionalist JJP Oud, as helping to
'organise a new *physis*' that would realise the utopia
envisioned by Scheerbart in his *Glass Architecture* of 1914.[7]

GLASS

In Scheerbart's fantasy treatise the material and technological inventions of his time were projected into a future
architecture as the necessary precondition for a new 'glass
culture' that would 'completely transform humanity'.[8]
Sharing the implicit environmental determinism that
marked various turn-of-the-century movements for the
reform of life, society and the means of production,
Scheerbart began his account of the anthropologically
transformative potential of glass walls, steel and concrete
structures, electric lighting, heating and cooling systems,
metal chairs, vacuum cleaners, cars, aircraft and floating
architecture by suggesting that 'if we want our culture to
rise to a higher level, we are obliged, for better or worse,
to change our architecture'.[9] If the current culture was
grown from an environment of closed rooms, then a new
culture, radically distinct from entrenched traditions,
requires that the closed character be removed from the
rooms in which people live. And this can only be achieved

91

by introducing glass architecture, 'which lets in the light of the sun, the moon, and the stars, not merely through a few windows, but through every possible wall, which will be made entirely of glass – of coloured glass.' The book's 111 sections – written in a straightforward, almost positivistic and technical language – outline the architectural characteristics of a future utopia that would be the legitimate heir to the extraordinary technical innovations of the nineteenth century.

In examining the achievements and weaknesses of surrealism, Benjamin was principally concerned with what he called 'the crisis of the intellectual …[and] the humanistic concept of freedom.'[10] Benjamin argues that the revolutionary intelligentsia had failed in its efforts not only to overthrow the rule of the bourgeoisie but even to make contact with the proletarian masses. Rather than perpetuate the intellectual's conception of contemplation as a revolutionary force, he suggested re-situating intellectual work in the sphere of images, which he would later theorise in terms of the distracted class consciousness of the proletariat. Consequently, the essay attempts to pull what Benjamin calls the trick of profane illumination from the surrealists' contemplative notion of experience as poetic, thus pushing life to the utmost limits of possibility. In order to correct the surrealists' 'pernicious romantic prejudices', Benjamin draws on Scheerbart's future vision of glass architecture, once directly and several times indirectly.

Where the French *literati* stand at the head of a powerful intellectual stream, intoxicated by poetic reverie, Benjamin describes himself as an outside observer who stands in the valley where he is able to gauge the energies of the movement and to calculate where, on this intellectual current, to install his power station. Seizing on André Breton's ability to transform the profane into illumination, Benjamin sought to generate a materialistic, anthropological kind of inspiration. Breton, Benjamin recounted, 'was the first to perceive the revolutionary energies that appear in the "outmoded", the first iron constructions, the first factory buildings, the earliest photos, the objects that have begun to be extinct'. No one before had 'perceived how destitution – not only social but architectonic, the poverty of interiors, enslaved and enslaving objects – can be suddenly transformed into revolutionary nihilism' … into revolutionary experience, if not action … [bringing] the immense forces of "atmosphere" concealed in these things to the point of explosion'. Early iron constructions attracted Benjamin's interest for their potential to be transformed into a revolutionary nihilism that would be capable of fulfilling the utopian dream of a glass culture.

The chemically explosive quality of profane illumination is linked to what Benjamin considered to be a radical theory of freedom. For the surrealists are, he wrote, 'the first to liquidate the sclerotic liberal–moral–humanistic ideal of freedom, because they are convinced that 'freedom, which on this earth can only be bought with a thousand of the hardest sacrifices, must be enjoyed unrestrictedly in its fullness without any kind of pragmatic calculation, as long as it lasts'.[11] While sharing this anti-humanist conception of freedom as moments of hard-won liberation rather than a new stable order, Benjamin remained careful to distance his ideas of profane illumination and revolutionary experience from what he calls the surrealists' 'inadequate, undialectical conception of the nature of intoxication'. He took issue with their 'histrionic or fanatical stress on the mysterious side of the mysterious', and contrasted Apollinaire's 'impetuous' and 'overheated embrace of the uncomprehended miracle of machines' to the 'well-ventilated utopias of Scheerbart'.

To transform the contemplative crucible of surrealist writing into a fully revolutionary thermodynamics, Benjamin presented the 'curious' dialectics of intoxication, whose structure, it seems, is homologous with that of 'revolution'. In addition to the opium eater, the dreamer and the ecstatic, he claimed that the reader, the loiterer and the *flâneur* are also types of *illuminati*. Moreover, he speculated that all ecstasy in one world is perhaps 'humiliating sobriety in that complementary to it.' Anxious to step 'into a world that borders not only on tombs of the Sacred Heart or altars to the Virgin, but also on the morning before a battle or after a victory,' he countered the delights of the Boulevard Bonne-Nouvelle in Breton's *Nadja* with the thought that 'living in a glass house [like living with the doors open] would be a revolutionary virtue *par excellence* … an intoxication, a moral exhibitionism, that we badly need'.[12] And in reply to Breton's proposition that 'mankind's struggle for liberation in its simplest revolutionary form … remains the only cause worth saving,' Benjamin posed the question 'But are [the surrealists] successful in welding this experience of freedom to the other revolutionary experience that we have to acknowledge because it has been ours, the constructive, dictatorial side of revolution? In short, have they bound revolt to revolution? How are we to imagine an existence oriented solely toward Boulevard Bonne-Nouvelle, in rooms by Le Corbusier and Oud?'[13] – rooms which Benjamin understood as materialising Scheerbart's rationalist dream, as containing traces of utopia.

At this point Benjamin notes that 'to win the energies of intoxication for the revolution – this is the project about which surrealism circles in all its books and enterprises.' To bind destruction and construction – enthusiasm and rationality – into a dialectic would be, as Benjamin comments in his notes for the *Arcades Project*, 'to encompass both Breton and Le Corbusier – that would mean drawing the spirit of contemporary France like a bow, with which knowledge shoots the moment in the heart.'[14] Here, he imagines the conjoining of these extremes as an instrument of cognition – a bow with which knowledge shoots 'the heart' – capable of producing what he elsewhere calls 'the Now of recognisability' where 'what has been within a particular epoch is always, simultaneously, "what has been from time immemorial".'[15] The idea of combining extreme rationality and extreme fantasy was both a topos in writings that took engineering as the paradigm for the new architecture and key to the shocking cognitive effects of Dada montage. The critic and historian Franz Roh, like Giedion a student of Heinrich Wölfflin, described montage in 1925 as a precarious synthesis of the two most important tendencies in modern visual culture – 'extreme fantasy with extreme sobriety (*Nüchternheit*).'[16] Alfred Meyer writes of the 'formative fantasy' of calculated engineering, 'here more reason, there more fantasy,'[17] while for Giedion the combination of rationality and vision in Garnier's 'Cité industrielle' leads him to prefer the more lasting effects of engineering to the momentary rush of cocaine.[18]

While Benjamin's dialectics of extreme polar opposites is not to be found in Scheerbart, there *is* a curious double-sidedness to his portrait of modern technology as both rational and enchanting, as there is in Meyer's introducing of the Crystal Palace (1851) by imagining a children's fable 'Of iron giants and glass maidens' and his suggestion that the glass pavilion at the Paris World's Fair of 1900 is a fairy tale come true.[19] In *Glass Architecture*, a text so dry that it is hard to read from beginning to end, Scheerbart intersperses practical suggestions and technical information with momentary revelations about the 'marvellous effects' of Tiffany glass; the 'splendour of glass palaces' with gardens paved in stone and majolica tiles that rival Arabian gardens; and the potential of producing 'glass brilliants [the size] of pumpkins,' because 'primitive people and children are enraptured by coloured glass.' And in a passage that combines the critical perspective of cultural theory, the pleasure of the fantasist and the indefatigable experimentalism of the inspired inventor, he writes,

We are not at the end of a cultural period – but at the beginning. We still have extraordinary marvels to expect from technics and chemistry, which should not be forgotten. This ought to give us constant encouragement. Unsplinterable glass should be mentioned here, in which a celluloid sheet is placed between two sheets of glass and joins them together.[20]

In Scheerbart's utopian dream, then, the rationality of technology and the enchantment of art coincide in a new paradigm combining the technological and the organic. This phenomenon is marked by the image of a glass milieu which would, according to the poet, have the potential to extend the psychological effects of Gothic stained glass and Babylonian glass ampullae to all realms of life, transforming homes into cathedrals with the same 'peculiar influence' that was already known to the priests of ancient Babylon and Syria. Through this secularisation of spiritual experience, 'a composed and settled nation' will emerge, blissful and healthy, its every desire already fulfilled.[21]

EXPRESSION

Benjamin's reading of modern architecture through Scheerbart's glass lens may seem surprising to students of twentieth-century architecture. Architectural historians have tended to associate Scheerbart exclusively with Bruno Taut and his Crystal Chain circle of the chaotic period at the close of World War I – expressionist fantasies of utopian cities among the mountains, exuberantly coloured buildings bursting and radiating with ecstasy, concrete flowing formlessly and steel suspended magically.[22] And, of course, Taut's privileged relationship with Scheerbart was marked by his dedication of his Glass House at the 1914 Werkbund exhibition in Cologne to Scheerbart, and Scheerbart's reciprocal dedication of his book *Glass Architecture* to Taut.[23] With its fountain streaming inside an ecstatic interior of coloured glass, encased like a precious seed in an outer shell of glass block, Taut's pavilion was to be a symbol – in the full Romantic sense of the term – for the renewal of 'organic' society. Similarly, Taut's friend the critic Adolf Behne had, in 1919, given Scheerbart's vision a leading role in what he hoped would be the 'return of art,' had criticised European humanism, valorised poverty and advocated the return to primitivism through which the creative power of the masses would awaken.[24] In doing so, he championed Taut, and to a lesser extent Walter Gropius, as the architects who promised to fulfil Scheerbart's vision. During the 1920s, it became characteristic of progressive architectural modernism in Germany to strive for the restoration of that pre-modern community, order and harmony that had been shattered by industrialisation and metropolitanisation, not by rejecting technology, but rather by (re)turning to nature – to the primitive and originary – through the most advanced building science and technology set in the open landscapes of the German garden cities, as exemplified by the *Siedlungen* of Berlin and Frankfurt-am-Main.

The implication of the expressionist desire to fuse the technical and the organic was not lost on Benjamin, whose reading of Scheerbart – like his reading of many others – involved transformative extensions and rewritings. While Benjamin used Scheerbart's vision of glass architecture in ways that contributed strategically to his theory of modern culture, he never referred to Bruno Taut or those preoccupations with the properties of colour, reflection and luminosity that Taut took from Scheerbart. In fact, Benjamin was antagonistic toward expressionism whose organicist hubris he associated with Fascism.[25] Where Behne considered architects like Taut capable of restoring the full unity of an organic society through industry, Benjamin considered the physiognomy of a redeemed future to remain radically unthinkable from what was already at hand. As he cautioned in concluding a review of Scheerbart's 'asteroid-novel' *Lesabéndio* (1913)

Art is not the forum for utopia. If it nevertheless appears that from the perspective of art the definitive word could be spoken about this book, because it is so full of humour, it is precisely this humour that exceeds the domain of art and makes the work into a testimony of spirit. The continued existence of that testimony is not eternal and is not grounded in itself, but will be sublimated into that greater (some)thing [*das Größere*] of which it is evidence. Of that greater (some)thing – the fulfilment of Utopia – one cannot speak, only bear witness.[26]

GESTALTUNG

Rather than Bruno Taut, Benjamin considered Le Corbusier, JJP Oud, Adolf Loos and the Bauhaus to be the architects who were 'realising' Scheerbart's ideas in what he took to be the most extreme rationalist and anti-organic architecture – architecture without 'art', governed by the spirit of pure engineering. Consistent with the polemical statements of the architects themselves, Benjamin understood their buildings to have realised the latent potential of industrial means of construction and new synthetic materials (glass, iron and concrete) finally liberated from the false bourgeois *Kultur* that had imposed the forms of previous historical epochs onto the 'new', enveloping them in myth throughout the nineteenth century.

While unexpected, Benjamin's interpretation of glass architecture should not be seen as a misreading of late-1920s modern architecture by an outsider from the literary world. Rather, his association in the mid-1920s with the extraordinary mixture of 'elementarist' avant-gardists around the magazine *G* may have given him an insight into the after-history of glass architecture that historians have generally overlooked. The magazine itself, produced through the studios of film-maker Hans Richter (who was principal editor) and architect Ludwig Mies van der Rohe (who contributed finance as well as articles and projects), assembled evidence of a new culture characterised by the multi-faceted notion of elementary *Gestaltung* (form-giving). This bridged a diverse array of post-expressionist artistic research, cut across disciplines and broke the barrier between art and engineering. Founded by Hans Richter and Viking Eggling, the original circle consisted of Hans Arp, Tristan Tzara, Ludwig Hilberseimer and Theo van Doesburg, but soon expanded to include Mies, El Lissitzky, Werner Graeff, Noam Gabo, Antoine Pevsner, Friedrich Kiesler, Georg Grosz, Man Ray, Walter Benjamin and Raoul Hausmann – embracing dadaists and neo-plasticists, constructivists and surrealists. Benjamin's translation of Tristan Tzara's short essay 'Photography from the Other

Side' appeared in issue 3 (June 1924) together with Mies's call for a more effective embrace of industrialisation for building through the invention of improved synthetic materials and the reorganisation of the trades to combine factory production of parts and on-site assembly that would realise the potential of rational 'montage' fabrication.[27]

Consider as well that as late as 1926, in an article on the properties, potentials and technical development of glass construction, Walter Gropius linked his newly completed Bauhaus building at Dessau to Scheerbart's vision when he wrote that 'Glass architecture, which was just a poetic utopia not long ago, now becomes reality unconstrained'.[28] In the previous year van Doesburg had also written of the significance of glass for bringing the new architectural image into harmony with the new needs and tempo of life, mentioning Gropius but singling out Loos and Kiesler in Austria, and Mies in Germany as being 'among the architects who, engrossed in the task of their times, try to innovate architecture in essence and in construction', leading the way to a new architecture that will be 'light, open, clear and, above all, temporary.'[29] Then again, van Doesburg's programme for his design of the House of an Artist for Léonce Rosenberg in 1923 navigated a Scheerbartian path between Le Corbusier's purism and Taut's utopian fantasy of Alpine architecture. 'Your atelier,' he writes to Rosenberg,

must be like a glass cover or like an empty crystal. It must have an absolute purity, a constant light, a clear atmosphere. It must also be white. The palette must be of glass. Your pencil sharp, rectangular and hard, always free of dust and as clean as an operating scalpel. One can certainly take a better lesson from doctors' laboratories than from painters' ateliers. The latter are cages that stink like sick apes. Your atelier must have the cold atmosphere of mountains 3000 metres high; eternal snow must lie there. Cold kills the microbes.[30]

Gropius himself had collaborated with Taut and Behne, both before the Great War and then afterwards; had called architecture 'the crystalline expression of man's noblest thoughts';[31] and had admired and enjoyed Scheerbart's writings, 'full of wisdom and beauty,' which he recommended to friends.[32] He also had hired Lyonel Feininger as one of the first masters of the Bauhaus in 1919 on the recommendation of Behne, who considered Feininger's paintings to be exemplary of his conflation of cubism and Scheerbart's utopia, the ultimate realisation of which would be architectural. While Feininger's medievalising crystalline woodcut for the first programme of Gropius' Bauhaus is well known, it should also be noted that Feininger's crystalline paintings and the transparent 'glass architecture' paintings of Moholy-Nagy were displayed in the Bauhaus exhibition of 1923, together with

László Moholy-Nagy, *Glass Architecture III*, 1921–22

Gropius' prismatic blocks for industrialised housing rendered on a Feiningeresque landscape.

It was this show that marked the celebrated 'turn' of the Bauhaus from expressionist elementarism to the functionalist constructivism for which it became most known (Gropius's 'synthesis of art and technology'), a turn marked most directly by Johannes Itten's departure and the arrival of Moholy-Nagy, who adopted the persona of the artist-as-engineer as well

as the cause of glass architecture. In the years immediately before this, Moholy-Nagy had deliberately realigned his work to Kasimir Malevich's crystalline suprematist paintings, on the one hand, and Adolf Behne's program-matic writings for a future cubist glass architecture. Beginning with the painting entitled *Glass Architecture*, which first appeared on the front page of the celebratory issue of *MA* of 1 May 1922, Moholy developed a distinctive preoccupation with transparency involving a complicated play of planes showing through one another, first in paintings, then photograms, lithographs, photographs, photocollages, stage sets and films, as well as the *Light–Space Modulator* (1922–30).[33] In 1929, Moholy concluded the summary statement of his Bauhaus pedagogy, *Von Material zu Architektur*, with a portrait of the emergent dematerialised transparent 'architecture' – a series of images that

Jan Kamman, 'Architecture', c. 1929

includes the same close-up of the Bauhaus at Dessau that Gropius had used for his 1926 article 'glasbau' and culminates in a negative multiple-exposure photograph by Jan Kamman of the Van Nelle Factory in Rotterdam (architects Brinkman & van der Vlugt), which Moholy describes as 'the illusion of spatial interpenetration, such as only the the next generation will possibly experience in reality – as glass architecture'.[34]

According to Oskar Schlemmer,[35] the influence of Berlin Dada on Gropius's shift in 1923 should also not be disregarded, nor, we might add, should van Doesburg's alter ego as a dadaist, nor the enthusiasm of the entire Dada circle for Scheerbart. The dadaists, too, had admired Scheerbart's writings, having formed themselves as a separate group out of the milieu of Herwath Walden's magazine *Der Sturm*, which had consistently brought Scheerbart's writings to the artistic community of Berlin before and during the Great War. In fact, the dadaists considered themselves to be the 'diapered children' of a new age and Scheerbart to be their spiritual father.[36] Hannah Höch had an extensive Scheerbart library. Raoul Hausmann and Johannes Baader renamed the Club Dada in March 1919 in homage to Scheerbart as 'Club zur blauen Milchstrasse.' The philosophers most associated with Dada – Anselm Ruest and Salomo Friedländer – contributed considerably to the interest in Scheerbart after the War. Even the 'Dada architect' Ludwig Hilberseimer wrote about him.

While the expressionists had invested their hope for

the renewal of organic wholeness in the figure of the New Man, whose deep inwardness was to provide the strength for a reconciliation with a troubled, fragmented and uncertain modern world, the dadaists rejected such transcendental and intoxicating subjectivity and reworked the New Man into an inorganic, historically and materially contingent figure who 'carries pandemonium within himself … for or against which no one can do anything.'[37] In photocollages, montages and assemblages – constructive techniques developed in opposition to the media of painting and sculpture – they portrayed the new subjectivity as internalising contradiction (rationality–fantasy; order–disorder) and living through the paradox of a technology born of nature but seemingly cast against it. And playfully, they recast themselves into fictional personae so as to re-enact satirically and critically the relationship of self to the structures of society and culture.

As early as September 1919, Hilberseimer cautioned against the misinterpretation of Scheerbart by expressionist architects, signalling a post-humanist line of research in the direction of Benjamin's later readings of Dada and glass architecture.[38] By 1920 Raoul Hausmann's conception of the New Man shifted from puppets to engineers as he began to portray constructors and technical drawings, practicality and conventionality as means to achieve a 'synthesis of spirit and matter,' which he called 'présentismus.'[39] In his 1922 'In Praise of the Conventional' he opposed the fantasy of 'artistes' with 'the fantasy of the technician, the constructor of machines … the scientific experimenter … the watchmaker, welder or locomotive engineer.'[40]

POVERTY

In Benjamin's essay of 1933, 'Experience and Poverty',[41] glass architecture assumes the characteristics of a revolutionary surface for a new subjectivity – an austere and slick surface on which it is hard to leave traces, accumulate commodities or form habits – a metaphor, perhaps an instrument, for Benjamin seeking to consider the possibility of beginning again at the beginning, as a potential of the catastrophic yet cleansing devastation of something like a war. The promise of modernity for Benjamin, writing on the eve of Hitler's proclamation of the Third Reich, was to be found paradoxically in the most abhorrent manifestations of inhumanity, in the impoverishment of experience brought on by the development of technology. With the prospect of war once again on everyone's lips, Benjamin chose to revisit the experience of the Great War – the first war of technology *and* the war that was to end all wars – in order to argue that this 'monstrous unfolding of technology,' with its capacity to destroy entire cities and erase all traces of the past, brought to mankind 'a wholly new impoverishment', a kind of barbarism whose destructiveness had a positive moment, eliminating 'the dreadful mishmash of styles and worldviews in the last century' to create a *tabula rasa* on which humanity was once again free of 'human experience in general', able to begin living again at the beginning. Where the expressionists had sought, after the devastation of the war, to renew the bourgeois ideal of organic and transcendental experience, Benjamin took this unprecedented destruction as an opening for the working masses to be freed of experience altogether, freed of preconceived cultural ideals as a child longs to be free of the received 'experience' of adults. These children of modernity 'yearn for an environment in which they can bring their poverty – the outward and ultimately their inward impoverishment as well – to such a pure and clear validity that something decent will come out of it'.

Paradoxically the erasure of 'experience' (*Erfahrung*) as something passed on had become necessary for the possibility of 'experience' (*Erlebnis*) in the sense of something lived – the elimination of history in exchange for the openness of historicity.[42] However, for Benjamin, any effort to restore experience in the organic sense remains problematic under capitalism. It is simply appropriated into the service of a false naturalism by a myth-making apparatus that in the process conceals the disquieting truths about capitalism. In the same way the experience of objects' auras has also been corrupted. Without relinquishing hope for the return of these lost experiences, but also without the pretence of depicting or creating them, Benjamin adopted a radically anti-organic perspective aimed at working through the problematic aspects of capitalism, industry and the technological environment that they were producing. As he indicated in the notes for the *Arcades Project*, 'The genuine liberation from an epoch … has the structure of an awakening in this respect as well: it is entirely ruled by cunning. Only with cunning, and not without it, can we work free of the realm of dream.'[43]

Passing in his text from the battlefield to modern architecture, Benjamin proposed a kind of 'traceless' living in a technologised environment that had realised itself fully, that is transparently, its physiognomy no longer deformed to harbour secrets. This image of glass links destruction and construction indissolubly and draws together the houses of modern architecture, a poem by Brecht, and portraits of a new post-humanist subject figured interchangeably as children, barbarians, engineers and the proletariat. Citing the refrain, 'Erase the traces!' from the first of Brecht's poems in 'From a Reader for Those Who Live in Cities' (1930), Benjamin writes: 'That was something for which Scheerbart with his glass and the Bauhaus with its steel have opened the way: they have created spaces in which it is difficult to leave traces'[44] – spaces that, together with telescopes, airplanes and rockets, were the precondition for transforming the humanity of the past into 'new creatures, worthy of notice and affection'. Brecht's poem provides a vivid image of a keen desire to escape bourgeois subjectivity. In order not to be caught, controlled or denounced in the modern metropolis of industrial capitalism, in order to slip past the codification of identity by friends, parents, habits, repeated thoughts and photographs, Brecht suggests taking cues from how the fugitive erases the traces of his life.

... If you meet your parents in Hamburg or elsewhere
Pass them like strangers, turn the corner, don't recognise them
Pull the hat they gave you over your face, and
Do not, O do not, show your face
Rather
Erase the traces!

... Whatever you say, don't say it twice
If you find your ideas in anyone else, disown them
The man who hasn't signed anything, who has left no picture
Who was not there, who said nothing:
How can they catch him?
Erase the traces![45]

In his essay on the impoverished poet of the Second Empire in Paris, Charles Baudelaire, Benjamin elaborated the problem of the bourgeoisie whose social system extends control ever further, prompting them to seek refuge in the privacy of their homes, where they become asocial and constitutionally resistant to control. For Baudelaire, however, the interior provided no refuge. Fleeing his creditors, he roved about continuously in the city that had long since ceased to be home to the leisurely flâneur.[46] For Benjamin's revolutionary subjects, erasing one's traces could become a paradigmatic form of resisting the growing network of social controls,[47] and at the same time playing at a modernity yet to come, just as children playing a game will always begin again at the beginning as if for the first time.[48] The bourgeois citizen, on the other hand, encased in the domestic interior with its accumulation of knick-knacks and habits, like the commodity whose utility was shrouded by myth, remained burdened with the hidden secrets of capitalist exploitation – alienation, poverty and the maniacal empathy of commodities.

Benjamin's reworking of Scheerbart's harmonious utopia into an image of glass as living without traces offers hope for working through these problematics at precisely the moment when the optimism of the Weimar republic, in its architecture as in its politics, was eclipsed by the rise of Fascism. From Dada to Brecht via the elementarism identified in *G*, Benjamin takes us to a milieu in which the tracelessness of the fugitive becomes an image for a groundless ground on which collective dreams pass into reality free of the resistance of history, culture and matter.

TRACES

In addition to nurturing the phantasmagoria of commodity fetishism, fashion and entertainment, what interested Benjamin about the Parisian arcades was that in them iron – a fully artificial building material – made its appearance for the first time in the history of architecture, having been developed in greenhouses, workshops and industrial structures. It was through the 'functional nature' of iron that 'the constructive principle began its domination of architecture', marking the shift within it from art to engineering, decorator to constructor, representation to presentation – a shift that had by Benjamin's time already entailed over a century of battles. For him that century was characterised by its *deficient* reception of technology,[49] by the production of images in which the old continued to intermingle with the new. He called these images 'wishful fantasies' in which 'the collective seeks both to preserve and to transfigure the inchoateness of the social product and the deficiencies in the social system of production'. These wish-fulfilling images (which is how Freud had characterised dreams) tend to direct the visual imagination 'back to the primeval past', thus linking their power of prophecy (for that which is to follow appears first in the images of dreams) to 'elements from prehistory, that is, of a classless society'. Intimations of a classless society, archived in the collective unconscious, mingle with the new 'to produce the utopia that has left its traces in thousands of configurations of life, from permanent buildings to fleeting fashions'.[50]

While the arcades had inspired the architectural form of Charles Fourier's utopian community (the phalanstery was imagined to be a city of arcades), Benjamin emphasised that Fourier's utopia was a 'reactionary modification' of the arcades into dwellings: simply 'the colourful idyll of Biedermeier' inserted into the austere, formal world of the Empire – a clear demonstration of how images in the collective consciousness intermingle the old with the new. Benjamin's conception of the dream-consciousness of the collective revolves around the problems and potentials that such interminglings pose for passage from the prehistory of modernity to a fully revolutionary state of redemption – to the return of origins, of prehistory in its other sense as ur-history, that paradise where living leaves no traces. For the dream likewise has a double sense, referring not only to utopias but also to the historical nightmare of capitalism from which it is necessary to awaken. For Benjamin, its essence is not any latent meaning or idealist form, but rather is constituted by the dream*work*. While Benjamin seems to have concurred in some ways with Max Weber's analysis of how Enlightenment rationality had 'disenchant-ed' the world, he also recognised that the modern world was not yet free of myth, for things produced as commodi-ties under the conditions of alienated labour were envel-oped by false mythologies, as evident in advertisements, fashion and architecture. 'Capitalism is a natural phenom-enon with which a new dream-sleep came over Europe, and, through it, a reactivation of mythic forces.'[51] These myths, as Georg Lukács had pointed out, gave the world of reified commodities the appearance and status of 'nature' – a second nature that occluded the original as it exploited it.[52] To awaken from the bad dream of capitalist phantasma-goria, to dissolve mythology into the space of history was Benjamin's primary motive for the *Arcades Project*, which he thought of – in terms similar to the work of dreams and dream analysis – as his *Passagenarbeit* or work of passage.[53]

The historical materialist in Benjamin considered awakening to occur in stages.[54] He believed that utopian projections such as those of Fourier or Scheerbart, as well as the work of related architects, would necessarily remain inadequate manifestations of the utopian impulse – the pulse of the original struggling to free itself from history. They could, nevertheless, be understood as moving in the direction of freedom through history (towards the Now of recognisability), through developments in the forces of production which – without forethought, let alone overt politics – 'reduced the wish symbols of the previous century to rubble even before the monuments representing them had crumbled.' This development of the forces of production in the nineteenth century, had

emancipated constructive forms from art, as the sciences [had] freed themselves from philosophy in the sixteenth. Architecture makes a start as constructional engineering. The reproduction of nature in photography follows. Fantasy creation prepares itself to become practical as commercial art. Literature is subject to montage in the feuilleton...[55]

In every sphere, the naturalist conventions of bourgeois art were displaced by the paradigm of technology and construction. And it was construction that in the nineteenth century served the role of the subconscious, as Benjamin quoted from Giedion's *Building in France*.[56] To be more precise, Benjamin's citation from Giedion should be read with his commentary in the *Arcades Project* where he attempted to rework Giedion's thesis in the following way: 'Wouldn't it be better to say "the role of bodily processes" around which "artistic" architectures gather, like dreams around the framework of physiological processes?'[57] Construction – *bauen* – then, as a kind of direct bodily production of labour, a potentially unmediated, collective physiological event in which dream-consciousness comes to realisation as 'traces in thousands of configurations of life...' Construction whose rationality progressively approaches transparency, whose physiognomy becomes increasingly an index of necessary material and social causes as developments in the forces of production, pursuing their own technical logic, bringing about the ruination of bourgeois culture and society. 'It is', he wrote, 'the peculiarity of *technological* forms of production (as opposed to art forms) that their progress and their success are proportionate to the *transparency* of their social content. (Hence glass architecture.)'[58] And elsewhere,

One can characterise the problem of the form of the new art straight on: when and how will the worlds of form, which have arisen without our assistance and which have subjugated us – in mechanics, for example, in film, in machine construction, in the new physics – make it clear what manner of nature they contain.[59]

Benjamin describes the arcades and bourgeois interiors, the exhibitions and panoramas of the nineteenth century as the 'residues of a dream world' at the beginning of the bourgeois epoch, as products of bourgeois class consciousness. They became a focus of his study, for in them he thought it was possible to glimpse the true face of prehistory. 'For us,' he noted, 'the enticing and threatening face of prehistory [*Urgeschichte*] becomes clear in the beginnings of technology, in the dwelling style of the nineteenth century; in that which lies closer to our time, it has not yet revealed itself'.[60] In the thousands of configurations of life, in the technology and dwelling style of his own time – in other words, in the residues of the collective dream world at the beginning of the proletarian epoch, at the beginning of the epoch of modern architecture – prehistory had not yet revealed itself.

Originally published in *Assemblage* 29, 7–23.

NOTES

1. The letter from Benjamin to Giedion, 15 February 1929, was until recently in the Giedion Archiv at the Institut für Geschichte und Theorie der Architektur of the ETH in Zurich. It is published in Sokratis Georgiadis' 'Introduction' to Sigfried Giedion, *Building in France. Building in Iron. Building in Concrete*, trans. J Duncan Berry (Santa Monica: The Getty Center for the Study of Art and the Humanities, 1995), 53.

2. Adolf Gotthold Meyer, *Eisenbauten* (Esslingen: Paul Neff, 1907).

3. Walter Benjamin, 'Bücher, die lebendig geblieben sind', *Gesammelte Schriften* (hereafter *GS*), 7 vols. (Berlin: Suhrkamp, 1970–), III:170. Here the word 'house' (*Haus*) could also mean building and construction; author's translation.

4. Giedion, *Building in France*, 167.

5. Ibid., 169.

6. Walter Benjamin copied the beginning of this citation in his notes for the *Passagen-Werk*. See Benjamin, *The Arcades Project*, trans. Howard Eiland and Kevin McLaughlin (Cambridge, MA: Belknap Press of Harvard University Press, 1999), 423 (M3a, 3).

7. See Walter Benjamin, 'Surrealism: The Last Snapshot of the European Intelligensia', translated by Edmund Jephcott in Walter Benjamin, *Selected Writings, vol. 2 1927–1934* (Cambridge, MA: Harvard University Press, 1999): 207–21. The reference to technology organising this *physis* is on page 217. Paul Scheerbart, *Glass Architecture*, trans. James Palmes (New York: Praeger, 1972), 74. Paul Scheerbart, *Glasarchitektur* (Berlin: 1914; Munich: Rogner & Bernhard, 1971). Several authors have explored Benjamin's reception of Scheerbart, most notably Pierre Missac in *Walter Benjamin's Passages*, trans. Shierry

Weber Nicholsen (Cambridge, MA: MIT Press, 1995), 147–72; John McCole, *Walter Benjamin and the Antinomies of Tradition* (Ithaca: Cornell University Press, 1993), 156–205; and Hubert Bär, *Natur und Gesellschaft bei Scheerbart. Genese und Implikationen einer Kulturutopie* (Heidelberg: Julius Groos Verlag, 1972). See also Detlef Mertins, 'Playing at Modernity', *Toys and the Modernist Tradition* (Montréal: Canadian Centre for Architecture, 1993), 7–16. It was Gershom Scholem who introduced Benjamin to Scheerbart on the occasion of Benjamin's wedding to Dora Sophie Kellner in 1917. Scholem recounts, 'I was a great admirer and collector of the writings of Paul Scheerbart, and as a wedding present I gave them my favourite books, Scheerbart's utopian novel *Lesabéndio*, which is set on the planetoid Pallas and, with Alfred Kubin's drawings, presents a world in which the "essential" human qualities have undergone complete transformation. This was the beginning of Benjamin's conversion to Scheerbart; three years later he made this book the subject of a major essay, "Der wahre Politiker" (The true politician), which unfortunately has not been preserved.' See Gershom Scholem, *Walter Benjamin. The Story of a Friendship* (New York: Schocken Books, 1981), 38.

8. Paul Scheerbart (1971), 137.

9. Ibid., 25.

10. Walter Benjamin, 'Surrealism. The Last Snapshot of the European Intelligentsia', *Reflections*, trans. Peter Demetz (New York: Harcourt Brace Jovanovich, 1978), 177–92; 'Der Surrealismus: Die letzte Momentaufnahme der europäischen Intelligenz', *GS* II (1), 295–310.

11. Ibid., 189.

12. Anthony Vidler has pointed to the complex relationship between this image of Benjamin's and that offered by Breton in *Nadja*: 'As for me, I continue to inhabit my glass house, where one can see at every hour who is coming to visit me, where everything that is suspended from the ceilings and the walls holds on as if by enchantment, where I rest at night on a bed of glass with glass sheets, where *who I am* will appear to me, sooner or later, engraved on a diamond.' See Anthony Vidler, 'Transparency', *The Architectural Uncanny. Essays in the Modern Unhomely* (Cambridge, MA: MIT Press, 1992), 218.

13. Ibid., 180, 181, 189.

14. Benjamin, *Arcades Project*, 459 (N1a,5).

15. Ibid., 464 (N4,1).

16. Franz Roh, *Nach-Expressionismus. Magischer Realismus. Probleme der neuesten europäischen Malerei* (Leipzig: Klinkhardt & Biermann, 1925), 46.

17. Meyer, 48, 4.

18. Giedion, 83, 77.

19. Meyer, 54, 153.

20. Paul Scheerbart, trans. James Palmes (1972), 44, 47, 66, 73.

21. Ibid., 72.

22. Many historical surveys – including Reyner Banham, *Architecture in the First Machine Age*, Kenneth Frampton, *Modern Architecture: A Critical History* and William Curtis, *Modern Architecture* – have been consistent with the more specialised treatments of Bruno Taut by Gustav Pehnt, Rosemary Haag Bletter and Iain Boyd Whyte, all of which stress the link between Scheerbart and Taut. While Whyte's *Bruno Taut and the Architecture of Activism* (Cambridge: Cambridge University Press, 1982) acknowledges the dadaists' admiration of Scheerbart (180), this receives only minor mention. Similarly, Regine Prange's *Das Kristalline als Kunstsymbol. Bruno Taut und Paul Klee* (Hildesheim: Georg Olms, 1991) does not discuss Dada, but provides a reference to Ludwig Hilberseimer's essay on Scheerbart (see note 34 below).

23. See Rosemarie Haag Bletter, 'Paul Scheerbart and Expressionist Architecture', *VIA* 8, 1986, 127–35, or her more extended treatment in *Bruno Taut and Paul Scheerbart's Vision: Utopian Aspects of German Expressionist Architecture* (New York: Columbia University Dissertation, 1973). Scheerbart's correspondence with Taut from December 1913 to February 1914 is published in Paul Scheerbart, *70 Trillionen Weltgrüsse: Eine Biographie in Briefen 1889–1915*, Mechthild Rausch, ed. (Berlin: Argon, 1992), 458–68.

24. Adolf Behne, *Die Wiederkehr der Kunst* (Berlin: Kurt Wolff, 1919).

25. See Benjamin's 'Karl Krauss', *Reflections*, 239–73; *GS* II (1), 334–67.

26. Benjamin, 'Paul Scheerbart: Lesabéndio', *GS* II (2), 618–20; author's translation.

27. *G: Material zur elementaren Gestaltung – Herausgeber Hans Richter 1923–1926*, ed. Marion von Hofacker (rpt. Munich: Der Kern, 1986). cf. Werner Graeff, 'Über die sogenannte G-Gruppe', *Werk und Zeit*, II (1962), 3–5, English translation, 'Concerning the so-called G Group', with introduction by Howard Dearstyne, *Art Journal*, 23:3 (Spring, 1994), 280–82; Raoul Hausmann, 'More on Group "G"', *Art Journal*, 24:4 (Summer 1965), 350–51. cf also Hans Richter, 'Dr Walter Benjamin', *Köpfe und Hinterköpfe* (Zurich: Der Arche, 1967), 87–88.

28. Walter Gropius, 'glasbau', *Die Bauzeitung*, 23 (1926) 20, 159–62; rpt. in Hartmut Probst and Christian Schädlich, eds., *Walter Gropius, Ausgewählte Schriften* (Berlin: Ernst & Sohn, 1988), 3:103–106.

29. Theo van Doesburg, '*Vernieuwingspogingen der Ooostenrijksche en Duitsche architectuur,*' *Het Bouwbedrijf*, 2:6 (June 1925) 225–27; 'The Significance of Glass; Toward Transparent Structures', trans. Charlotte I Loeb and Arthur L Loeb, *Theo van Doesburg, On European Architecture. Complete Essays from Het Bouwbedrijf 1924–1931* (Basel: Birkhäuser, 1990), 63–69.

30. Quoted in A Elzas, 'Theo van Doesburg', *De 8 en Opbouw* 6 (1935), 174; cited and translated by Nancy Troy, *The De Stijl Environment* (Cambridge, MA: MIT Press, 1983), 106.

31. Walter Gropius in an untitled pamphlet on the occasion of the Exhibition for Unknown Architects organised by the Arbeitsrat für Kunst, 1919.

32. Letter from Walter Gropius to Hermann Finsterlin, 17 April 1919, cited in Marcel Franciscono, *Walter Gropius and the Creation of the Bauhaus in Weimar: The Ideals and Artistic Theories of its Founding Years* (Chicago: University of Illinois, 1971), 124, 156.

33. For a fuller account of Moholy-Nagy's relationship to the disembodied utopia of Adolf Behne and the work of his 'glass architecture period', see Krisztina Passuth, *Moholy-Nagy* (London: Thames & Hudson, 1985), 22–27.

34. László Moholy-Nagy, *Von Material zu Architektur* (1929, rpt. Mainz: Florian Kupferberg, 1968), 236.

35. Oskar Schlemmer, 'The Staatliche Bauhaus in Weimar, 1923', trans. Wolfgang Jabs and Basil Gilbert in Hans M Wingler, *The Bauhaus: Weimar Dessau Berlin Chicago* (Cambridge MA: MIT Press, 1969), 65–66.

36. For an account of Club Dada as a 'Scheerbart society', see Hanne Bergius, *Das Lachen Dadas. Die Berliner Dadaisten und ihre Aktionen* (Gießen: Anabas Verlag, 1989), 42–47. Much of this confusion stems from the ambiguity of 'Expressionism' as an art-historical category, which Paul Fechner's book *Der Expressionismus* (Munich: R Piper & Co, 1914) brought into usage designating a broad array of modern painting, distinguished only from cubism and futurism. Thus, when Herwath Walden called Scheerbart 'the first Expressionist' (see 'Paul Scheerbart', *Der Sturm*, 6 (1915), 96), he established a line of interpretation that remained unaffected by the subsequent formation of Berlin Dada and its claim to the legacy of Scheerbart.

37. Richard Huelsenbeck, 'Der neue Mensch', in *Neue Jugend* I (1917), 2.

38. Ludwig Hilberseimer, 'Paul Scheerbart und die Architekten', *Das Kunstblatt*, 3:9, September 1919, 271–73. In his review of Arthur Korn, *Glas im Bau und als Gebrauchsgegenstand* (1926) and Konrad Werner Schulze, *Glas in der Architektur der Gegenwart* (1929) of 1929, Hilberseimer reiterated his rationalist interpretation of Scheerbart's visionary utopia and claimed that it had anticipated the widespread use of construction in glass by the late 1920s. See Ludwig Hilberseimer, 'Glas Architektur', *Die Form*, 1929, 521–22. Post-humanism in architecture was first identified and analysed by K Michael Hays, *Modernism and the Posthumanist Subject: The Architecture of Hannes*

Meyer and Ludwig Hilberseimer (Cambridge, MA: MIT Press, 1992).

39. Raoul Hausmann, 'Présentismus', in *Raoul Hausmann, Texte bis 1933*, ed. Michael Erlhoff, (Munich: Texte + Kritik, 1982), vol. 2, 25–26.

40. Raoul Hausmann, 'Lob des Konventionellen', ibid., 49.

41. Walter Benjamin, 'Erfahrung und Armut', *GS* II (I), 213–19.

42. At the same time, Benjamin insists consistently on the concreteness of historicity, explaining that what distinguishes his notion of images from 'the "essences" of phenomenology is their historic index. (Heidegger seeks in vain to rescue history for phenomenology abstractly, through "historicity".)' Benjamin, *Arcades Project*, 173 (N 3,1).

43. Benjamin, *Arcades Project*, 173 (G,1,7).

44. Benjamin, 'Erfahrung und Armut', 217; author's translation.

45. Bertolt Brecht, 'Ten Poems from a Reader for Those Who Live in Cities', in John Willett & Ralph Mannheim, eds., *Bertolt Brecht Poems* (London: Eyre Methuen, 1976), 131–50. Bertolt Brecht, 'Aus dem Lesebuch für Städtebewohner', *Versuche*, vol. 2 (Berlin: Gustav Kiepenheuer, 1930).

46. Walter Benjamin, *Charles Baudelaire. A Lyric Poet in the Era of High Capitalism*, trans. Harry Zohn (London: Verso, 1976) 47. *GS* I (2), 511–604.

47. Ibid., 47.

48. For a fuller treatment of Benjamin's writings on toys, play and new beginnings see Detlef Mertins, 'Playing at Modernity' (note 7 above).

49. See for instance Walter Benjamin, 'Eduard Fuchs, Collector and Historian', in Edmund Jephcott and Kinsley Shorter trans., *One-Way Street and Other Writings* (London: NLB, 1979), 358.

50. Benjamin, 'Paris, Capital of the Nineteenth Century', *Reflections*, 147–48. 'Paris, die Hauptstadt des XIX. Jahrhunderts', *GS* V, 45–60.

51. Benjamin, *Arcades Project*, 391 (K1a,8).

52. Georg Lukács, 'Reification and the Consciousness of the Proletariat', *History and Class Consciousness* (Cambridge, MA: MIT Press, 1971). Originally published in 1922.

53. Richard Sieburth makes the distinction between *Passagenwerk* and *Passagenarbeit* in Sieburth, 'Benjamin the Scrivener', in Gary Smith, ed., *Benjamin: Philosophy, Aesthetics, History* (Chicago: University of Chicago Press, 1983), 26.

54. Benjamin, *Arcades Project*, 388 (K1,1).

55. Benjamin, 'Surrealism', 161.

56. Giedion, 3.

57. Benjamin, *Arcades Project*, 858 (Oo,8).

58. Ibid., 581 (N4,6). Walter Benjamin, 'N' [Re the Theory of Knowledge, Theory of Progress], trans. Leigh Hafrey and Richard Sieburth, in Gary Smith ed., *Benjamin: Philosophy, History, Aesthetics* (Chicago: University of Chicago, 1989), 58.

59. Benjamin, *Arcades Project*, 396 (K3a, 2).

60. Ibid., 393 (K2a, I). Translation slightly revised.

WALTER BENJAMIN AND THE TECTONIC UNCONSCIOUS: USING ARCHITECTURE AS AN OPTICAL INSTRUMENT

Long accustomed to the concept of tectonics as a nonrepresentational, even anti-representational foundation for architectures of resistance or poetics of authenticity, I was surprised a few years ago to read Mitchell Schwarzer's scholarly portrayal of Karl Boetticher's mid-nineteenth-century tectonics as a theory of representation.[1] Schwarzer reopened a topic that had seemed closed, but even more importantly, he went on to isolate one of the thorniest issues of representation – the relationship between self-representation and difference (alterity). Schwarzer's presentation of Boetticher's tectonics centred on the hermeneutic problem of architectural ornamentation or 'representation' seeking to interpret the raw 'ontological' moment in which artifice is created out of unformed matter. More recently, in a panel discussion with Schwarzer, the literary theorist and critic Julian Patrick pointed out that this tectonic problematic of 'authentic' representation was after all structured by a rhetorical trope – that of the chiasmus, struggling constantly to bridge the unbridgeable gap between self and other, known and unknown, conscious and unconscious, in order to stabilise representations that are prone to coming apart. Patrick's observation, possible only by expanding the frame of reference beyond architecture's internal discourse, suggests that the theory of tectonics could benefit from contemporary cross-disciplinary investigations into the problematics of representation.

Despite their apparent overexposure, the writings of Walter Benjamin include appropriations and transformations of modernist architectural history and theory – including Boetticher's tectonics – that provide a hinge between discourses of modernism and post-structuralism. This essay focuses on three moments in his writings that touch on the issue of representation in a different way: first, Benjamin's reading of Boetticher's tectonics as a theory of history in which the unconscious serves as a generative and productive source that challenges the existing matrix of representation; secondly, Benjamin's transformation of Sigfried Giedion's presentation of iron structures as optical instruments for glimpsing a space interwoven with a collective unconscious, the image of which had seemingly been captured by a certain kind of photography; and thirdly, Benjamin's suggestion that the mimetic faculty continues to play a role within representation, history and technology in order to produce similarities between the human and the non-human. In each instance, Benjamin reworked the dynamic dualism of nineteenth-century architectural tectonics – (self)representation seeking reconciliation with alterity – into a dialectic. In so doing, he set the cause of revolution (of a modernity yet to come) against metaphysical and utopian claims, progressive and regressive alike.

TECHNICAL FORMS

In the opening segment of his well-known exposé for the *Arcades Project* of 1935 – 'Paris, Capital of the Nineteenth Century' – Benjamin referred to the architect and historian Karl Boetticher, and he was not flattering.[2] He associated Boetticher with what he elsewhere referred to as the nineteenth century's deficient reception of industrial technology, that is, the problematic production of images in which the old persists and intermingles with the new. He called these 'wish images' in which 'the collective seeks both to overcome and to transfigure the immaturity of the social product and the inadequacies in the social system of production'. Benjamin explained that, Janus-like, such wish-fulfilling images (which is how Freud had characterised dreams) tended to direct the visual imagination 'back upon the primal past', thus linking their power of prophecy (for that which is to follow appears first in the images of dreams) to 'elements of primal history – that is, to elements of a classless society'. Intimations of a classless society, achieved in the collective unconscious, mingle with the new to produce 'the utopia that has left its traces in a thousand configurations of life, from enduring edifices to passing fashions'. Benjamin offered Charles Fourier's utopian vision of a community housed in a phalanstery as such an image, combining promise and problematics. He considered its architecture a 'reactionary metamorphosis' of the arcades into 'the colourful idyll of Biedermeier', inserted into the austere, formal world of the Empire.

For Benjamin, it was the destiny of the working masses to realise the non-instrumental potentiality of industry and yet the latent physiognomy of technical forms remained constrained under the rule of the bourgeoisie, just as the workers were themselves. Concurring with Max Weber's analysis of how Enlightenment rationality had 'disenchanted' the world, he nevertheless recognised that modernity was not yet free of myth. Things produced as commodities under the conditions of alienated labour were enveloped by false mythologies, as evident in advertise-ments, fashion and architecture. 'Capitalism', he noted in the *Arcades Project*, 'is a natural phenomenon with which a new dream-sleep came over Europe, and in it, a reactivation of mythic powers'.[3] These myths, to which Georg Lukács had drawn attention to as being characteristic of the class consciousness of the bourgeoisie, gave the world of reified commodities the appearance and status of 'nature' – a second nature that occluded the original as it exploited it.[4]

To awaken from the nightmare of capitalist phantas-magoria – to dissolve mythology into the space of history – was Benjamin's principal aim for the *Arcades Project*, which he thought of, in terms similar to the work of dreams and dream analysis, as his *Passagenarbeit* or work of passage. In Jeffrey Mehlman's apt formulation, 'Benjamin's work on the phantasmagoric glass and iron arcades of Paris constituted a devastating enactment of the messianic dream of plunging into evil, albeit to defeat it from within'.[5] Benjamin's reading of modern architecture and photography during the late 1920s in Germany (*neues Bauen* and *neue Optik*), like his reading of their histories, was informed by these problematics of dream-consciousness – the resistance posed by the old for passage across the threshold of modernity into an undistorted and fully revolutionary state of redemption.

Having noted in the exposé that the emergence of construction in iron was critical for the appearance of the sky-lit and gas-lit Parisian arcades during the fashion boom around 1820, Benjamin referred to Boetticher's conviction that the art forms of the new system of iron construction must follow the formal principle of the Hellenic mode. Benjamin went on to describe the Empire style, which conformed to Boetticher's prescription, as being the equivalent in architecture to 'revolutionary terrorism' in politics, for which 'the State is an end in itself'. Invoking a kind of functionalism against the politics of historicism, which served to legitimate the present by reiterating the forms of the past, he wrote:

Just as Napoleon failed to understand the functional nature of the state as an instrument of domination by the bourgeois class, so the architects of his time equally did not grasp the functional nature of iron, with which the constructive principle begins its domination of architecture. These architects design supports resembling Pompeian columns, and factories that imitate residential houses, just as later the first railroad stations will be modelled on chalets.[6]

That Benjamin sided with the engineer against the architect is clear from the first part of the exposé, in which he suggested that engineering had a revolutionary role to play, not only for architecture but for society. Having already introduced this theme in his essay 'Surrealism' of 1929 and again, more radically, in 'Erfahrung und Armut'

('Experience and Poverty') of 1933, Benjamin returned
to it at the end of the exposé. There he took up what he
called the surrealists' gaze across 'the ruination of the
bourgeoisie' and observed:

**The development of the forces of production shattered
the wish symbols of the previous century, even before
the monuments representing them had collapsed. In
the nineteenth century this development worked to
emancipate the forms of construction from art, just as
in the sixteenth century the sciences freed themselves
from philosophy. A start is made with architecture as
engineered construction.**[7]

By linking 'artistic' architecture to the phantasmagoria
of bourgeois capitalism, while at the same time linking
'engineering' architecture to social revolution, Benjamin
radicalised and politicised the conflict between engineering
and architecture that had marked the nineteenth century.
He drew it into the overarching dialectical struggle
between the classes and the new and old.

In this context, Benjamin's reading of Boetticher's
tribute of 1846 to Karl Friedrich Schinkel takes on a rather
strategic significance for the dialectical theory of
architecture that may be glimpsed between the lines of
his writings. It was, of course, in this text – 'The Principles
of the Hellenic and Germanic Ways of Building with
Regard to their Application to our Present Way of
Building'[8] – that Boetticher had extended his theory of
tectonics to the matter of iron. Having previously analysed
the two great historical styles – the trabeated Hellenic
system and the vaulted Germanic-Gothic – he turned to
speculate on the architecture of the future, the new
architecture that so many in the nineteenth century longed
for so intensely. In the notes of the *Arcades Project*, Benjamin
assembled the following excerpts:

**Another art, in which another static principle establishes
a tone even more magnificent than that of the other two,**

will struggle the womb of time to be born ... A new and unprecedented ceiling system, one that will naturally bring in its wake a whole new realm of art forms, can ... make its appearance only after some particular material – formerly neglected, if not unknown, as a basic principle in that application – begins to be accepted. Such a material is ... iron, which our century has already started to employ in this sense. In proportion as its static properties are tested and made known, iron is destined to serve, in the architecture of the future, as the basis for the system of ceiling construction; and with respect to statics, it is destined to advance this system as far beyond the Hellenic and the medieval as the system of the arch advanced the Middle Ages beyond the monolithic stone-lintel system of antiquity ... If the static principle of force is thus borrowed from vaulted constructions and put to work for an entirely new and unprecedented system, then, with regard to the art forms of the new system, the formal principle of the Hellenic mode must find acceptance.[9]

For Boetticher, the new iron architecture had a double origin – structure pursuing a 'new and hitherto unknown system', while art assimilated the new with the old principles of antique form. In his earlier writings, Boetticher had introduced the twin notions of *Kernform* and *Kunstform* (technical form and art form) precisely to account for what he took to be the necessary relationship between material origins and idealised re-presentations of material properties and structuring forces in Hellenic and Gothic architecture. This relationship was central to his understanding of architectural style *per se*, as an integrated system of production and symbolisation. He conceived of unmediated material and structural self-expression on the one hand, and interpretative self-representation through ornament on the other, as mutually mediating and hence indivisible. In transposing this historical schema into the future, into his speculations about the physiognomy of a new iron architecture, he clearly hoped to promote the emergence of an equally integrative architectonic system for the new epoch.

Yet in positing the split between nature and culture as a condition of modernity, Boetticher inscribed into his tectonic theory an unending struggle to maintain their mutuality over the process of historical development. In linking 'technical form' and 'art form' to the opposition between Germanic and Hellenic styles, Boetticher had hoped to draw on the integrative strength of his dualism in order to forge a new and higher architecture through *stylistic* synthesis, but his strategy may have had the opposite effect. It merely confirmed the split that was becoming increasingly apparent and freed the impulse for a new structural principle from the obligation to represent itself through the mediation of old tectonic systems.

Benjamin's brief commentary on these passages reveals that he took Boetticher's notion of a double origin as a sign of conflict rather than the complementary relationship that Boetticher had intended. Subtly reworking Boetticher's dualism, Benjamin noted that his history demonstrated the '*dialectical* derivation of iron construction' (emphasis added).[10] In so doing, Benjamin was informed by Alfred Gotthold Meyer's prior reworking of tectonic theory in his posthumously published *Eisenbauten (Iron Constructions)* of 1907.[11] Benjamin held Meyer's book in the highest esteem, calling it a 'prototype of materialist historiography'.[12] He singled it out in 1929 as one of four books that had 'remained alive', the others being Alois Riegl's *Late Roman Art Industry* (1901), Franz Rosenzweig's *The Star of Redemption* (1921), and Georg Lukács' *History of Class Consciousness* (1923).

In his book, Meyer had been critical of the Berlin tectonic school inaugurated by Schinkel, for its insistence that traditional forms and principles of architectonic expression, developed for stone and wood, be used to assimilate iron construction into the art of architecture. Instead, Meyer adopted engineering as the vital and dynamic basis of a new architecture that would grant to technical forms the potential of a new self-generated beauty. Where Boetticher found, in 1846, that the various

efforts to 'shake off the shackles of the past' had not yet
achieved persuasively original art forms *or* structural
systems, Meyer spoke of the Eiffel Tower of 1889 in terms
of a 'new beauty, the beauty of steely sharpness' and the
expression of a new tempo of tectonic vitality. While
Boetticher argued that 'the acceptance and continuation
of tradition, not its negation, is historically the only correct
course for art ... leading it toward the destined emergence
from tradition to a newborn, original, and unique style,'
Meyer's later more *sachlich* and anti-representational
approach to the relation between art and iron technology
was distinguished by his refusal of any wilful symbolisation. Instead he favoured the supposed immediacy of
material properties, calculations, purposes and modes
of production. He conceived of beauty as the immanent
expression not only of the material but of the society
that produced it. Where Boetticher feared what remained
outside the system of order, Meyer embraced the rush
and terror of the technological sublime.[13]

While rejecting Boetticher's prescription for contemporary architecture, Meyer and Benjamin both reiterated
aspects of the theory of history that underpins his tectonics, in which material and structural innovations are seen
to emerge from a mysterious source – 'the womb of time'
– to play a leading role in the formation of a new system.
For Boetticher, a new structural system specific to a new
material was to be born out of the old in the same way that
a distinctive and integral Roman vaulted architecture had
emerged out of the Hellenic through a process of hybridisation, mutation and rationalisation. Meyer, too, was interested in the unknowable source of new architectures, but
instead of Boetticher's metaphors of birth and metamorphosis, Meyer suggested that a new style is always precipi-
tated by an 'unconscious urge' and that 'any generation
destined to create a new style ... (will) need to start the
process of formal creation from the beginning.'[14] In the
case of iron construction, the drawing board of rational
engineering calculations and structural diagrams constituted such a new beginning, with the path to formal

self-realisation moving from elementary to complex and from part to whole. In 'Experience and Poverty', Benjamin likewise mobilised the blank rationality of the engineer's drawing board as a groundless ground for a new (proletarian) society, for starting again at the beginning, albeit within the phantasmagoria. In the exposé, he referred to construction as the 'subconscious of the nineteenth-century', taking the phrase not from Meyer but from the young architectural historian Sigfried Giedion, whose book of 1928, *Building in France – Building in Iron – Building in Ferro-Concrete*,[15] Benjamin admired almost as much as Meyer's.[16]

Conflating metaphors of organic growth and subconscious impulses, Giedion held that the new forms of iron construction – and the new forms of life (mass society) that emerged with them – began as kernels struggling within the old, gradually to assume their own identity. His story of the historical passage of iron construction follows a morphological evolution – from the simple iron roof frame of the Théâtre Français of 1786 to the full realisation of iron's potential in the vast spans and gracefully engineered arcs of the Palais des Machines of 1889. This natural progression was, in his portrayal, hindered by the persistence of tradition among architects, until the twentieth century, when they finally took up the task of bringing what had emerged in the dark subconscious of industrial labour into the clarity of a self-conscious architectural system, distinguished by a new kind of spatial experience.

Benjamin's quotation of Giedion's thesis about construction as the subconscious of the epoch may be considered in relation to a pair of images that Giedion used graphically to present what he took to be the line of development from the glass facade of an exhibition hall of 1848 to the curtain wall of Walter Gropius's Bauhaus at Dessau of 1925–26 – the technical form 'finally' purified, refined and self-reflexive. But it should also be read in conjunction with Benjamin's commentary on it. He suggested: 'Wouldn't it be better to say "the role of bodily processes" around which "artistic" architectures gather, like dreams around the framework of physiological processes?'[17] In reworking Giedion's dualism into a dialectic between physiological processes and phantasmagoric dreams, Benjamin pointed to the immanence of truth within the expression of bodily labours and the physiognomy of historical events. This immanence, however, remained impeded by bourgeois controls, albeit less in the technical realm (unworthy of bourgeois attention) than in the artistic.

The architecture of emerging mass society could, then, be seen as beginning not only in the corrupt form of the bourgeois arcades but also in the less deficient forms of utilitarian structures – engineered bridges, train stations, grain silos, exhibition halls and, of course, the factory, the nascent home of workers and engineers. 'It is', Benjamin wrote, invoking Boetticher's terms, 'the peculiarity of *technological* forms of production (as opposed to art forms) that their progress and their success are proportionate to the *transparency* of their social content. (Hence glass architecture.)'[18] Even in the technical realm, Benjamin treated this transparency as mediated – historically, materially and perceptually. With respect to the artistic realm, he suggested: 'One can characterise the problem of the form of the new art straight on: when and how will the worlds of form, which have arisen without our assistance and which have subjugated us – in mechanics, for example, in film, in machine construction, in the new physics – make it clear what manner of nature they contain?'[19] When and how, in other words, would construction – pursuing its own inherent logic of purification, working within but against the system of production, working within but against the object riddled with error – bring about the ruination of bourgeois culture and society, and do so without overt politics but rather through a collective physiological labour that had the character of a constantly renewed uprising?

OPTICAL INSTRUMENTS

By considering tectonics within the problematics of
representation, Benjamin was able to both clarify and
radicalise the terms of the tectonic discourse, while
functionalist architects and historians of his generation
merely eschewed representation, confident of their capacity
to step beyond it and materialise the elemental primitive-
ness of utopia in the here and now of white prismatic
volumes, curtain walls and cantilevered slabs. For Benjamin, the process of physiognomic immanence freeing itself
from distorting mediations was not only incomplete but
could not, in fact, be fulfilled by humanity alone. In seeking
to conjoin radical messianic Judaism and revolutionary
historical materialism, he considered such redemption
contingent on superhuman intervention. The hope and
even excitement that Benjamin revealed in describing the
arcades, exhibitions and panoramas of the nineteenth
century as 'dream houses of the collective'[20] at the beginning of the bourgeois epoch came from a conviction that in
them it was possible to glimpse the true face of prehistory,
which remained opaque in the artefacts of his own time, at
the beginning of the epoch ushered in by the proletariat.
He noted, 'the enticing and threatening face of prehistory is
clearly manifest to us in the beginnings of technology … it
has not yet shown itself in what lies nearer to us in time.'[21]

Benjamin's historicised theory of technological
productivity in the field of architecture underscores the
significance of metaphors of passage for his theory of
history. At the same time, it sets up another constellation
of metaphors concerning a new optics – the expansion of
vision made possible by modern technologies including
iron structures that provided unprecedented views of the
city, glimpses perhaps of the 'enticing and threatening face
of prehistory' yet to come. As is well known, Benjamin's
'Artwork' essay of 1935–39 introduced the idea that an
equivalent analytical practice had emerged in the realm of
the visual to psychoanalysis in the realm of the psyche.
Sigmund Freud's *Psychopathology of Everyday Life*,[22] Benja-

min observed, had 'isolated and made analysable things which had previously floated unnoticed on the broad stream of perception. A similar deepening of apperception throughout the entire spectrum of optical – and now also auditory – impressions has been accomplished by film.'[23]

The technique that Benjamin singled out to exemplify how 'through the camera … we first discover the optical unconscious, just as we discover the instinctual unconscious through psychoanalysis'[24] was the close-up – the blow-up, the enlargement, the cropped image, the fragment. 'With the close-up', he observed, 'space expands'.[25] Moreover, the

enlargement [of a snap-shot] not merely clarifies what we see indistinctly 'in any case', but brings to light entirely new structures of matter … Clearly, it is another nature which speaks to the camera as compared to the eye. 'Other' above all in the sense that a space interwoven with human consciousness gives way to a space interwoven with the unconscious.[26]

Such a space interwoven with unconsciousness was palpable for Benjamin, who consistently located the unconscious in the material world itself, not outside, behind, above or below it, but within – as he did the 'truth content' of the work of art and 'traces' of prehistory. In his first essay on surrealism, 'Traumkitsch' (Dreamkitsch) of 1925, he distinguished the analytics of the surrealists from those of Freud precisely for tracking down 'the traces not so much of the soul as of things'.[27] For Benjamin, truth was hidden from casual observation, but resided in traces within the welter of base material. He considered it the task of criticism, like the task of history, to make fragments of truth visible and dominant. Regardless of medium, he considered criticism an activity of stripping its objects bare, mortifying them, dragging the truth content of what is depicted in the image out before it, not as 'an unveiling that destroys the mystery but a revelation that does it justice'.[28] Thus the negativity and destructiveness of criticism opens up a moment of revelation, which in turn opens the future potentiality of the object. This notion of potentiality was related to Benjamin's proposition that phenomena have a natural history, that their nature lies in the full and concentrated scope of that history – in their pre-history as well as their present state. The idea that this natural history could be fulfilled may be understood within Benjamin's thought as approaching his hope for redemption from yet another perspective.

In the 'Artwork' essay, Benjamin was concerned with the problem of the work of art in the modern industrial epoch, distinguished not only by mechanical reproducibility but by phantasmagoria and commodity fetishism. In this context, Benjamin's concern for the intermingling of old and new focused on the perpetuation, into the era of capitalism, of the old phenomenon of aura, which he defined as a uniqueness that, in earlier times dominated by ritual, had enveloped the work of art as 'the unique apparition of a distance, however near it [the object] may be'.[29] During the nineteenth century, the phenomenon of aura had become an agent of bourgeois mythology working to maintain dominance over the masses. Without such constraint, he suggested, the class consciousness of the masses would tend to destroy aura as a function of a desire 'to "get closer" to things spatially and humanly'.[30] The photographic image enabled them to get hold of an object at close range, prising it (in its objectivity) from its aural encasement. Elsewhere, he wrote of other tactics for achieving similar ends, proceeding eccentrically and by leaps to rip things out of context in order to highlight the seemingly inconsequential details of larger structures ignored by the dominant class; and inventing a *historiographic telescope* capable of seeing through the phantasmagoric fog – a haptic–optical instrument for bringing the tangible, tactile concreteness of things closer to view.[31]

Just as psychoanalysis treats dream images as rebuses or picture puzzles whose manifest content must be deciphered, so Benjamin discovered in the photographic close-up a technique for reading latent content *within* the manifest, for seeing hidden significance *within* the surface. But what was it that he hoped to see? Perhaps justice with respect to the past; repressions and oppressions worked through; the object or event released to fulfil its mysterious potentiality; the enticing and threatening face of prehistory.[32] And how might this have appeared? In his 'Surrealism' essay of 1929, he suggested that 'we penetrate mystery only to the degree that we recognise it in the everyday world, by virtue of a dialectical optic that perceives the everyday as impenetrable, the impenetrable as everyday'.[33] Perhaps these were the effects of the close-up that he had in mind when, in a well-known passage of the 'Artwork' essay, he wrote that the moment of the close-up bursts open the prison-world of the everyday metropolis, the milieu of the proletariat – the bars and city streets, offices and furnished rooms, railroad stations and factories that 'seemed to close relentlessly around us … so that now we can set off calmly on journeys of adventure among its far-flung debris'.[34]

Benjamin left several concrete clues to the kind of (impenetrable) images that he associated with such adventurous travelling. Twice in the notes of the *Arcades Project*, he recorded his interest in Giedion's photographs of the Pont Transbordeur in *Buildings in France*. His letter to Giedion, a few weeks following the publication of the 'Surrealism' essay, reveals the strong affinity that he felt for

Sigfried Giedion, Pont Transbordeur spanning the industrial harbour of Marseilles

Giedion's historiography – his admiration for what he called Giedion's 'radical knowledge'. In the *Arcades Project*, he wrote that 'just as Giedion teaches us to read off the basic features of today's architecture in the buildings erected around 1850, we, in turn, would recognize today's life, today's forms, in the life and in the apparently secondary, lost forms of that epoch'.[35]

Familiar with the discourse of the new optics (led in the late 1920s by Giedion's friend László Moholy-Nagy),

Benjamin took this ability to read the future in the past as contingent on a new technologically mediated vision. Implicitly, he affiliated this with the tactics developed by the surrealists to produce profane illuminations, glimpses of a sur-reality within the banal experiences of everyday life – within, for instance, the extraordinary iron and glass structures of nineteenth-century Paris. One of Benjamin's notes begins by citing Giedion's 'encounter' with the 'fundamental aesthetic experience of today's building' in the 'windswept stairwells of the Eiffel Tower, and even more in the steel supports of the Pont Transbordeur ... (where) things flow through the thin net of iron spanning the air – ships, sea, houses, masts, landscape, harbour lose their definition: swirl into one another as we climb downward, simultaneously commingling'. He then went on to note that the 'magnificent vistas of the city provided by the new construction in iron ... for a long time were reserved exclusively for the workers and engineers'.[36] Elsewhere he continued, 'For in those days who besides the engineer and the proletarian had climbed the steps that alone made it possible to recognize what was new and decisive about these structures: the feeling of space?'[37]

While similar structures had been built in Rouen, Nantes and Bordeaux, it was the swaying, hovering and dizzying Pont Transbordeur, built by the engineer Ferdinand Arnodin in 1905 across the industrial harbour of

Sigfried Giedion, View from the Pont Transbordeur of a street alongside the industrial harbour of Marseilles

Marseilles, that assumed special significance among the avant-garde. Giedion observed how this 'balcony springing into space' – photographed by Moholy-Nagy, Germaine Krull, Herbert Bayer, Man Ray and others – had entered the unconscious of modern architecture in Germany.[38] In his words, 'The "new architecture" has unconsciously used these projecting "balconies" again and again. Why? Because there exists the need to live in buildings that strive to overcome the old sense of equilibrium that was based only on fortress-like incarceration'.[39]

Giedion had even featured the astonishingly delicate yet bold 'transporter', built to carry a small ferry across the harbour without interfering with the boats, on the cover of *Building in France*. His photographs, as well as his words, treat its spatial and optical effects (like those of the earlier Eiffel Tower) as paradigmatic of the emerging epoch. Of course, Meyer had already taken exciting images of technology, such as the bridge over the Firth of Forth, as demonstrating that 'the power of [iron] speaks to us and in us in every great train station and exhibition hall, in front of every great iron bridge and in the fast-paced modern metropolis'.[40] Giedion also mobilised a rhetoric that echoed the aesthetics of the sublime, but not as aesthetics. Invoking dematerialisation, spatial extension, shadowless light, and air as a constitutive material, he revelled in the fluid and gravity-free interweaving of subject and object and in the unsettling movement, formlessness and metamorphosis engendered by the pulse of life in iron structures. Both Meyer and Giedion eschewed bourgeois aesthetic categories, and instead treated these new spatial experiences as the structural conditions of the emerging era. For them, technology's transformation of buildings into fleshless open bodies of skeletal transparency, like its transformation of the nature of vision with microscopes, telescopes, aerial photography and X-rays, marked the emergence of new modes of perception, cognition and experience specific to the emerging era.

Hovering weightlessly and breathlessly above the harbour of Marseilles, Giedion's 'iron balcony' served to reframe and shatter the familiar, harsh world of the industrial metropolis, providing Benjamin with a graphic image of the 'threshold' of awakening from the false dream-consciousness of the bourgeoisie. It is telling that Benjamin focused on photographs by Giedion that were quite distinct from his dizzying and destabilising images of the Eiffel Tower, which Giedion had described as the first instance of the montage principle and exemplary of the tendency of the new structures to 'open themselves to all kinds of possibilities', to blur the boundaries of their autonomy in favour of relationships and interpenetrations in which the subject is united with the object in the creative process of space-formation. Instead, by selecting abstracted, fragmented close-up views of the harbour's edge taken from the top of the structure and through its open frame-work, Benjamin effectively distinguished between two moments in Giedion's thinking: one Benjamin identified as 'radical knowledge' serving historical self-consciousness and justice; the other enthusiastically proclaimed that a new immediacy had already arrived under the sign of a vitalist, technologically mediated transparency where 'there is only one great, indivisible space in which relation-ships and interweaving rule instead of fixed borders'. Benjamin focused not on images of the great iron structures themselves but on the unprecedented views of the city that they afforded. Among Giedion's photographs, only the ones singled out by Benjamin treated the view as mediated, and only in them was the unacknowledged misery of working-class life both revealed and simultaneously transformed into a site of revelation, just as they had been in Moholy-Nagy's constructivist film *Marseille, Vieux-Port* of 1929.

While Benjamin admired the rationalised technical forms of these montage structures (he also referred to the Eiffel Tower as the first instance of montage), he focused on their role as viewing instruments. Their web-like structures provided opportunities to crop, cut, reframe and abstract the familiar. Like the lens of a camera, they could reveal hidden secrets and provide glimpses of the estranged within the city of representation, 'the tiny spark of contin-gency, of the here and now, with which reality has (so to speak) seared the subject'.[41] Benjamin called these views glorious, for they released something of a magnificent potentiality locked within the reality of alienation and exploitation. With Giedion's camera and the power of the close-up to expand space and reveal secrets, Benjamin collapsed Boetticher's tectonic dualism, transforming the hermeneutics of origins into an immanence within representation whose visibility in the present was, however, contingent on technology's most powerful instruments of optical analysis. To open the object riddled with error, Benjamin mobilised a dialectical optics that

on the one hand, film furthers insight into the necessities governing our lives by its use of close-ups, by its accentuation of hidden details in familiar objects, and by its exploration of commonplace milieux through the ingenious guidance of the camera; on the other hand, it manages to assure us of a vast and unsuspected field of action (*Spielraum*).[42]

MAGICAL SIMILARITIES

The effects attributed by Benjamin to the Pont Transbordeur bear a striking resemblance to his treatment of photographs by David Octavius Hill, Karl Dauthendey and Karl Blossfeldt in his essay 'Little History of Photography' of 1931.[43] The fact that a portion of this is repeated verbatim in the section of the 'Artwork' essay that deals with the power of close-ups to explode the experience of the metropolis invites a reading of Giedion's photographs in terms parallel to Benjamin's reading of these other images. In this way, a third reformulation of the tectonic problematic may be inferred from his writings.

In his essay on photography, Benjamin suggested that, in contrast to painting, with photography 'we encounter something new and strange'.[44] His interest was captured, to begin with, by one of the numerous calotypes that Hill had made of fishwives, fishermen and children in Newhaven, Scotland, between 1843 and 1847. Unlike the precision and fidelity of the more expensive daguerreotypes, the soft orange-brown and sepia calotypes, with their diffuseness and transparency, were considered by some the most engaging and truly artistic medium, and came to be admired for their power to evoke personality, to find the presence below the surface, to probe behind appearances. Referring to Hill's portrait of Mrs Elizabeth Hall, Benjamin observed:

in Hill's Newhaven fishwife, her eyes cast down in such indolent, seductive modesty, there remains something that goes beyond testimony to the photographer's art, something that cannot be silenced, that fills you with an unruly desire to know what her name was, the woman who was alive there, who even now is still real and will never consent to be wholly absorbed into 'art'. And I ask: 'How did the beauty of that hair, those eyes, beguile our forebears? How did that mouth kiss, to which desire curls up senseless as smoke without fire?' [45]

To underscore his concern for the immediacy of lived experience, as captured by the photographer in a tense relationship with his own artful idealisations, Benjamin turned briefly to a picture by Karl Dauthendey, a German post-mortem photographer of the late nineteenth century living in Moscow at the time the photograph was taken. Benjamin's description invokes an image of Dauthendey himself, together with the woman to whom he was engaged, lying in the bedroom of his home, shortly after the birth of her sixth child. Her arteries were severed and her gaze absorbed in 'an ominous distance'. The silent violence of this image is both shocking in relation to Hill's and revealing of the unconscious realm that Benjamin saw opened up by the new optics. With these photographs already in mind, Benjamin then continued:

Immerse yourself in such a picture long enough and you will realise to what extent opposites touch, here too: the most precise technology can give its products a magical value, such as a painted picture can never again have for us. No matter how artful the photographer, no matter how carefully posed his subject, the beholder feels an irresistible urge to search such a picture for the tiny spark of contingency, of the here and now, with which reality has

(so to speak) seared the subject, to find the inconspicuous spot where in the immediacy of that long-forgotten moment the future subsists so eloquently that we, looking back, may rediscover it. *For it is another nature that speaks to the camera than to the eye: 'other' in the sense that a space interwoven with human consciousness gives way to a space interwoven with the unconscious ... It is through photography that we first discover the existence of this optical unconscious, just as we discover the instinctual unconscious through psychoanalysis.* **Details of structure, cellular tissue, with which technology and medicine are normally concerned – all this is, in its origins, more native to the camera than the atmospheric landscape or the soulful portrait. Yet at the same time photography reveals in this material the physiognomic aspects, image worlds, which dwell in the smallest things – meaningful yet covert enough to find a hiding place in waking dreams, but which, enlarged and capable of formulation, make the difference between technology and magic visible as a thoroughly historical variable.**[46]

Adding yet a third image to this constellation, Benjamin turned to the 'astonishing' plant photographs of Professor Karl Blossfeldt, designer and teacher at the United States Schools of Free and Applied Art in Berlin. The images appeared in Blossfeldt's book of 1928, *Art Forms of Nature,*[47] together with an introduction by the gallery owner Karl Nierendorf, whose thoughts share certain affinities with Benjamin's own – thoughts on the 'unity of the creative will in nature and art' (vi); their respective embodiment of a profound sublime secret; 'joining the two poles of the Past and the Future' (iii); and how the modern techniques of photography and film as well as microscopes and astronomical observatories 'bring us into closer touch with Nature than was ever possible before, and with the aid of scientific appliances we obtain glimpses into worlds which hitherto had been hidden from our senses'.[48] Paraphrasing Nierendorf, Benjamin wrote that Blossfeldt's uncanny photographs

reveal the forms of ancient columns in horse willow, a bishop's crosier in the ostrich fern, totem poles in tenfold enlargements of chestnut and maple shoots, and gothic tracery in the fuller's thistle. Hill's subjects, too, were probably not far from the truth when they described 'the phenomenon of photography' as still being 'a great and mysterious experience' – even if, for them, this was no more than the consciousness of 'standing before a device which in the briefest time could capture the visible environment that seemed as real and alive as nature itself'.[49]

At the risk of being reductive, condensing Benjamin's eloquently woven thoughts may help to register more emphatically the link between these various ideas: that the most precise technology can give its products a magical value; that the photographic enlargement can reveal a secret within the physiognomic surface of things; that that secret is visible in a tiny spark of contingency with which reality has seared the subject, in inconspicuous spots where in the immediacy of that long-forgotten moment the future subsists so eloquently that we, looking back, may recognise it – and recognise it as another nature, one interwoven with unconsciousness. All of this makes possible a great and mysterious experience, an experience of the natural within the human and the human within the natural; an experience whereby the difference between technology and magic is seen to be strictly historical, implying not only their commonality, but also a future potentiality.

That magic – the correspondence between the natural and human – has a history and that this was subsumed into the history of technology was most explicitly treated by Benjamin through the concept of similarity in his essays 'Doctrine of the Similar' and 'On the Mimetic Faculty', both of 1933.[50] There he described how humanity's special gift for seeing and producing similarities between the human and non-human has a history that is both phylogenetic and ontogenetic – that is, a history within the species that parallels its history within the life of each of its members. In other words, this faculty changes over the course of historical development as it does over the life of each person. Just as 'children's play is everywhere permeated by mimetic modes of behaviour … the child plays at being not only a shopkeeper or teacher but also a windmill and a train',[51] so in other essays Benjamin characterised the proletariat as the new-born children of the emerging industrial age, whose games always try to begin again at the beginning.[52]

While it appears that the mimetic faculty has decayed over time, that 'the perceptual world [*Merkwelt*] of modern human beings seems to contain far fewer of those magical correspondences than did that of the ancients or even that of primitive peoples',[53] Benjamin suggested that this faculty has, rather, been transformed into a *non*-sensuous similarity, now borne exclusively by language. 'This bearer is the semiotic element [of language]. Thus, the nexus of meaning of words or sentences is the bearer through which, like a flash, similarity appears.'[54]

However, Benjamin's apparent exclusion of the sensuous here needs to be qualified by the dependence of language on the sensuous media of speech and script, just as flames rely on substances that burn. Notwithstanding his emphasis on modern semiotic language, Benjamin also treated modern technologies of mechanical production and reproduction – photography and film, glass and iron – as bearers of correspondences between the human and the non-human. Benjamin's concept of similarity concerned the effects of things as much as their attributes. As technical forms that had been reduced to the limit of their objectification, these media (like the sober technical language that Benjamin admired in Bertolt Brecht and Paul Scheerbart) held the special potential of not only materialising similarity in their elemental form, but bringing the similarity hidden in other things into momentary visibility. They were instruments capable of producing glimpses, which the snap of the shutter, the dynamite of the tenth-of-a-second, was able to rip from the flesh of history and preserve.[55]

Believing that every epoch dreams its successor, Benjamin was especially attentive to utopian schemes. One of his earliest versions of the *Arcades Project* was even named after an image by the French humourist JJ Grandville, from his 1843 satire of modernist utopias, *Another World*.[56] In his précis of 1928–29 'The Ring of Saturn or Something about Iron Construction', Benjamin suggested that a small cosmic vignette by Grandville might demonstrate, in the form of a grotesque, the infinite opportunities that the nineteenth century saw opened up with construction in iron. Focusing on the adventures of a small goblin trying to find his way around in space, Grandville's story was accompanied by an etching that depicts an iron bridge with gas lanterns springing from planet to planet in an indefinite perspective, an unending passage into the infinite depths of space. The 333,000[th] pillar, we are told, rests on Saturn, where the goblin sees that the ring of this planet is nothing but an iron balcony on which the inhabitants of the planet take the evening air. Preceding Boetticher's text on iron by two years, and the Crystal Palace by nine, the bridge and balcony are remarkably modern and free of historical stylisation. Later, in the exposé of 1935, Benjamin still included this image in the section on 'Grandville, or the World Exhibitions', calling it a 'graphic utopia'.

To be able to commune with the cosmos, to link the past and future, to produce similarities between representation and alterity without restriction – such could be the opportunities of technology and industrialisation pursued rationally to their ultimate potential beyond the exploitation of nature under capitalism. However, let us remember that this image of absolute unity and openness was a satire of utopians such as Fourier and the Saint-Simonians, that Benjamin admired the satire of Karl Kraus which 'creeps into those he impersonates in order to annihilate them'[57] and that he concluded his tribute to the utopian fantasist Paul Scheerbart, written in the final months of his life, by recalling that 'art is not the forum of utopia … Of that greater (some)thing – the fulfilment of Utopia – one cannot speak, only bear witness'.[58]

Originally published in *ANY* 14 (1996), 28–35.

NOTES

1. Mitchell Schwarzer, 'Ontology and Representation in Karl Boetticher's Theory of Tectonics', *Journal of the Society of Architectural Historians* 53 (September 1993), 267–80.

2. Walter Benjamin, *Arcades Project*, trans. Howard Eiland and Kevin McLaughlin (Cambridge, MA: Belknap Press of Harvard University Press, 1999), 3–13.

3. Ibid., 391 (K la, 8).

4. Georg Lukács, History and Class *Consciousness*, trans. Rodney Livingstone (Cambridge, MA: MIT Press, 1971).

5. Jeffrey Mehlman, *Walter Benjamin for Children: An Essay on the Radio Years* (Chicago: University of Chicago Press, 1993), 80.

6. Benjamin, *Arcades Project*, 4; translation altered slightly.

7. Ibid., 13.

8. Karl Boetticher, 'Das Prinzip der hellenischen und germanischen Bauweise hinsichtlich der Übertragung in die Bauweise unserer Tage', *Allgemeine Bauzeitung*, 2 (1846): 111–25; Carl Gottlieb Wilhelm Boetticher, 'The Principles of the Hellenic and German Ways of Building', *In What Style Should We Build? The German Debate on Architectural Style*, trans. Wolfgang Herrmann (Santa Monica: Getty Center for the History of Art and Humanities, 1992), 147–67.

9. Benjamin, *Arcades Project*, 150 (F1,1).

10. Ibid.

11. Alfred Gothold Meyer, *Eisenbauten: Ihre Geschichte und Ästhetik* (Esslingen: Paul Neff, 1907).

12. Walter Benjamin, *Gesammelte Schriften* (henceforth GS), 7 vols.,

(Berlin: Suhrkamp, 1970–), III:170.

13. In his introduction to the English translation of Sigfried Giedion's *Bauen in Frankreich*, Sokratis Georgiadis observed that 'What Meyer experienced as non-aesthetic, he actually described in terms of an aesthetic of the sublime', 35.

14. Meyer, *Eisenbauten*, 115.

15. Sigfried Giedion, *Bauen in Frankreich: Bauen in Eisen – Bauen in Eisenbeton* (Leipzig & Berlin: Klinkhardt and Biermann, 1928; *Building in France: Building in Iron – Building in Ferro-Concrete*, trans., J. Duncan Berry (Santa Monica, CA: The Getty Center for the Study of Art and the Humanities, 1995).

16. For a more detailed treatment of Benjamin's reading of Giedion and Meyer, see the preceding essay in this volume.

17. Benjamin, *Arcades Project*, 858 (Oo,8).

18. Ibid., 465 (N4,6).

19. Benjamin, *GS*:V (K3a,2); translation based on that in *Arcades Project*, 396.

20. Benjamin, *Arcades Project*, 405 (LI,3).

21. Ibid., 393 (K,2a,1); translation altered slightly.

22. Sigmund Freud, *The Psychopathology of Everyday Life*, trans. Alan Tyson (New York : WW Norton, 1960).

23. Walter Benjamin, *Selected Writings* (henceforth *SW*), 4 vols., eds. Howard Eiland and Michael W Jennings (Cambridge, MA: Harvard University Press), 4:256.

24. Ibid., 4:266.

25. Ibid., 4:266.

26. Ibid., 4:266. I have altered the translation of this passage to render Benjamin's use of '*durchwirken*' as 'interweaving' rather than 'inform'.

27. Benjamin, *GS* II.2:621–22.

28. Benjamin, *GS* I.1:211/*OT*, 31.

29. Benjamin, *SW* 4:255.

30. Ibid.

31. Benjamin, 'Benjamin an Kraft. Paris, 28.10.1935' (*GS* V.2,1151).

32. Eduardo Cadava has given a more precise reading of this in 'Words of Light: Theses on the Photography of History', *Diacritics* 22 (1992), 84–114.

33. Benjamin, *SW* 2:216.

34. Benjamin, *SW* 4:265/*GS* I.2:499–500)

35. Benjamin, *Arcades Project*, 458 (N1,11).

36. Ibid., 459 (N1a,1).

37. Ibid., 156 (F3,5). The significance of these notes was first recognised by Susan Buck-Morss in *The Dialectics of Seeing: Walter Benjamin and the Arcades Project* (Cambridge, MA: MIT Press, 1989).

38. See exhibition catalogue, *Le pont Transbordeur et la Vision Moderniste* (Marseille: Musées de Marseille, 1991).

39. Giedion, *Building*, 147.

40. Meyer, *Eisenbauten*, 5.

41. Benjamin, *SW* 2:510.

42. Benjamin, *SW* 4: 265.

43. Benjamin, *SW* 2:507–30/*GS* II.1:368–85.

44. Benjamin, *SW* 2:510.

45. Ibid.

46. Ibid., 2:510–12. Emphasis added. I have altered the translation by Edmund Jephcott and Kingsley Shorter by using the more palpable phrase 'interwoven with consciousness' instead of their 'informed by'.

47. Karl Blossfeldt, *Kunstformen der Natur* (Berlin: Ernst Wasmuth, 1928); *Art Forms in Nature* (New York: E. Weyhe, 1929).

48. Karl Nierendorf, 'Art Forms in Nature', in Blossfeldt, *Nature*, iii–xiii.

49. Benjamin, *SW* 2:512.

50. Walter Benjamin, 'Doctrine of the Similar' trans. Michael Jennings (*SW* 2:694–98)/ 'Lehre vom Anlichen' (*GS* II.1, 204–10). 'On the Mimetic Faculty', trans. Edmund Jephcott (*SW* 2:720–22)/ 'Über das mimetische Vermögen' (*GS* II.1, 210–13).

51. Benjamin, *SW* 2:694.
52. See Detlef Mertins, 'Playing at Modernity', in *Toys and the Modernist Tradition* (Montreal: Canadian Centre for Architecture, 1993), 7–16.
53. Benjamin, *SW* 2:695.
54. Ibid., 722.
55. Ibid., 696–98.
56. JJ Grandville, 'Une Autre Monde', in *Bizarreries and Fantasies of Grandville* (New York: Dover Press, 1978).
57. Walter Benjamin, 'Karl Kraus', translated by Edmund Jephcott, in Walter Benjamin, *Selected Writings, vol. 2, 1927–1934* (Cambridge, MA: Harvard University Press, 1999): 431–57. Quotation is on page 442.
58. Walter Benjamin, 'Paul Scheerbart: Lesabendió', in *GS* II.2, 618–20.

SAME DIFFERENCE

During the early 1980s, in the heyday of the post-modern reaction against late modernism, the critic Demetri Porphyrios portrayed Crown Hall (1950–56), Mies van der Rohe's school of architecture at the Illinois Institute of Technology, as an architecture of total control and discipline. He called it 'homotopic', requiring everything and everybody to conform to the grid of universal rationality, to the geometry that organised the building into a unified totality. 'It was as if, by gridding space,' he wrote, 'one safeguarded against all accidents or indiscreet intrusions, and established instead an idealised field of likeness'.[1] Instead of Mies's 'immaculate homogeneity', Porphyrios promoted Alvar Aalto's work for what he called its 'heterotopic' ordering sensibility. The individual parts of Aalto's Wolfsburg Cultural Centre (1958), for instance, were each given their own differentiated form in relation to their function, and were arranged into assemblages whose unity was seen to be open and inclusive.

Porphyrios' interpretation was inspired by Michel Foucault's critique of the universalising claims of humanism and his call instead for 'heterotopias', such as the incongruous taxonomy of animals that Borges recounts from a 'Chinese encyclopedia'.[2] Foucault explained that where utopias offer the dream of a common locus or structure beneath all things, the heteroclite disturbs by secretly undermining language, destroying the syntax that causes words and things to hold together. However, where Foucault emphasised the capacity of heterotopias to corrode sameness and promote difference, Porphyrios focused on the forms of Aalto's heterogeneous collage. In retrospect, Aalto's ordering sensibility appears to have produced representations of difference rather than de-territorialisations that enable difference to emerge. Fixed and inflexible, Aalto's forms crystallised activities that were scripted in advance; an auditorium is an auditorium and an office is an office. In contrast, Foucault did not specify the form of heterotopia, but rather described its effects.

In this respect, it is worth recalling Mies's critique of Hugo Häring's organ-like functionalism in the 1920s. Where Häring wanted each part of his building to serve its intended function so precisely that a hallway would become narrower as it reached its end where fewer people would use it, Mies suggested that this limited the range of possible uses. Instead, he sought to achieve durability over time by making generous spaces that could serve a range of functions, even ones unforeseen. 'The purposes for which a building is used', he contended, 'are constantly changing and we cannot afford to tear down the building each time. That is why we have revised Sullivan's formula "form follows function" and construct a practical and economical space into which we fit the functions'.[3] Mies's pursuit of universal space implies, not a narrow conception of function, but a generous and open-ended approach to living, albeit within the structuring logics of industrial production and mass society that he accepted as givens to be worked through.

If we look not only at Mies's forms but also at the ways of life that they engendered, his pursuit of the universal within the historical conditions of the modern epoch takes on the character of a relentlessly destabilising strategy within the practice of architecture and even within his own work as well. Throughout his career, Mies set his architecture against the perpetuation of old habits and in the service of emergent and experimental ways of doing things. In working on the Weissenhofsiedlung in 1926, he hoped to 'open a new land' in which house and garden were merged into a fluid architectonic continuum that supported the *Lebensreform* ideal of living as much outdoors as in. On another occasion, he spoke of providing 'a ground for the unfolding of life', suggesting that the architect be a catalyst for the process of becoming. Later, in America,

Mies's empty glass boxes – the 'neutral frames' that were not entirely neutral after all – provided an infrastructure for the production of difference. This is what Alison and Peter Smithson sensed in their appreciation of the 'recessive' and 'loving neutrality' of Mies's late work, which they linked to a 'new kind of light-touch inhabitation'.[4] Mies wanted every person, like every building, to be free to realise their own immanent identity; for him, the aim of order was to bring together self-generated individualities without impinging on that freedom.

With its long-span structural system set on a 10-foot bay, Crown Hall was the only building at IIT that deviated from the 24-foot campus grid, which was based on the optimal size for a classroom. Perhaps the absence of classrooms in the architecture school suggested the deviation, but there were also no lecture halls or faculty offices. Instead, there was a single large room – 120 feet by 220 feet by 18 feet high, raised above the ground, and enclosed entirely by glass walls, translucent below and transparent above. It is in this space that the life of the school continues to unfold, subdivided only minimally by a multi-purpose space in the centre. The open studio maximises flexibility and the opportunity of shared experiences, enabling students to be aware of everything and participate fully. Focused inward yet extending out to the sky, the building is a catalyst for community within and connectivity beyond. It provides a lightly structured field for quotidian life and special events, calm yet alive, its rhythm changing over the course of the day and through the year, unified yet open.

The central space has served for formal lectures, exhibitions and events, including the memorial service for Mies and, recently, a wedding. It is also used for informal gatherings, pin-ups of student work, mock-ups of floor plans, construction of large models, and simply hanging out. With rows of individual desks, the orderly regime of the studios is offset by an ad hoc manner of teaching and collaborative work. Professors gather students informally around someone's desk to talk about their work or wheel in chalk-boards as needed, with students sitting randomly on their boards or stools. Large models appear as needed and conversations erupt wherever drawings are pinned up or students work together. For the annual open house, as well as special occasions, the entire space is reconfigured into an exhibition hall. A few years ago, the central area was even carpeted with Kentucky blue grass. In 1958, a major concert by Duke Ellington turned Crown Hall – 'the fish bowl of Tech' – into a ballroom with coloured spotlights for 900 'smiling faces'.[5] Recently, the experimental musical ensemble, MASS, transformed the building into a giant stringed instrument, with 24,000 feet of high-polish brass wire transferring vibrations directly into the steel structure.

What makes Mies's universal space universal is not the grid, after all, which is simply one of several ordering devices and only appears strongly in the rendered plan, but the singularity of the large and largely unstructured room – an architecture that Mies described as 'almost nothing', a void sandwiched between two uninterrupted horizontal

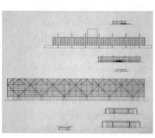

Office of Mies van der Rohe, elevations for seven clear-span buildings drawn to uniform scale

planes in which anything, everything and nothing can happen. Its relative emptiness transforms the iron cage of industrial rationality into an enabling device for emergent social formations and unforeseen events. Operating within but against the regime of the mass, Mies's universal space staged the uprootedness so central to the experience of modernity, as both a crisis and an opportunity for self-fashioning. Like Walter Benjamin's image of glass architecture as a milieu for a mode of dwelling that leaves no traces, Mies's glass boxes provoke an existential approach to life, drawing the occupant back to the blankness and potentiality of new beginnings, over and over again, promoting self-determination within yet against the world, while safeguarding alterity.

But what of the uniformity and repetition of Mies's work, building after building? To begin, Mies distinguished himself among the architectural avant-gardists precisely by *not* projecting a total vision for a new utopian society or city. Nevertheless, his work – especially in America – shares in the dream of a common locus or structure beneath all things that Porphyrios associated with utopia. It is this dream that gives Mies's work its consistency and rigour, a dream fuelled by the scientific literature that he read, beginning with the physics of Pierre-Simon Laplace (1749–1827), who sought to account for all phenomena across the terrestrial, molecular and celestial scales in terms of one principle, the forces of attraction and repulsion between particles. The idea of a universal principle governing all of creation had become a central theme in the seventeenth century when a secular theology emerged, transforming the principle of God's homogeneous presence in the universe into a scientific postulate linked to a belief in humanity's capacity to hasten redemption through self-discipline and reform. The desire to reunite humanity with the Godhead was transformed into a programme of reintegration in nature, seeking to align humanity with the governing principles of creation as revealed by science.

The goal of reintegration was powerfully re-articulated around 1900 by the zoologist Ernst Haeckel, who invented the science of ecology and popularised a monistic world-view in which society, politics and the arts were to be modelled after nature. Haeckel discovered radiolarians, tiny microscopic sea creatures composed of the most primitive elements, and presented them as exemplars for art and design. The simplicity of the radiolarians was understood to be key to their multiplicity and universality, for they could assume an infinite variety of beautiful forms and adapt to different environments all over the world. Ever more powerful microscopes and telescopes confirmed the principle of structural homogeneity from the microscopic to the macroscopic while demonstrating the capacity of nature to produce an infinite variety of wondrous forms.

This combination of homogeneity of structure with

heterogeneity of individuation was reiterated throughout
the twentieth century by scientists and by artists, architects
and engineers eager to use science to fuel new invention.
More recently, the sciences of complexity have updated
this quest, once again providing new models that, in
concert with new technologies, have inspired architects
such as FOA. Over the past decade, the work of FOA has
consistently explored the possibility of a new architectural
paradigm – at once mathematical, spatial and technological
– that would correspond to the order of nature (as best
we know it) and, like nature, sponsor the proliferation
of difference.

Notwithstanding his expressed desire to establish a
new language that could be broadly shared by others, Mies
developed a corpus of work characterised by restless
striving, experimentation, variation and refinement. A
drawing from the 1960s compares the elevations of seven
clear-span buildings at the same scale, revealing just how
diverse these buildings really are. Different in size, from
the tiny Farnsworth House and 50 x 50 House to the
gargantuan Convention Hall (720 feet square), they are also
different in structure, employing both one-way and
two-way spanning systems, expressed alternatively above
or below the roof, with overhangs or without. They all use a
modular grid, yet its dimension varies, as does that of the
structure. Similar yet different from one another, these
buildings cannot be reduced to the static model of
industrial standardisation or to a schema. If the specificity
of programmes, clients, sites and local conditions accounts
for much of their diversity, what is it then that unites them?
While the idea of type might be helpful, it would have to be
a dynamic conception of type, such as Goethe developed in
his morphology of plants.

Consider a selection of leaves from the field buttercup
(*Ranunculus acris*), arranged from the bottom of the stem to
the top. Despite its extensive range, the series nevertheless
gives the impression of an overall unity. No one leaf,
however, suffices as a measure or model for all the others.[6]
Rather, their unity remains implied, contingent on the

Leaves from the field buttercup
(*Ranunculus acria*)

progression and transformation of the series, on what Goethe called the metamorphosis of the plant – 'the process by which one and the same organ presents itself to us in manifold forms'.[7] This unity remains open to the possibility that a new form will take its place among the others and inflect the series. So, too, the form of Mies's long-span pavilions presents itself to the mind only through the progression of examples, as a generative field of movement or a form-making movement that leads to and from the resultant object. Because the unity of this movement-form includes other members of the series, it is constantly becoming other in order to remain itself. Its identity is founded precisely on the potential to be otherwise, demanding that the visible form be superseded again and again in an endless production of sameness and difference.

Originally published in Foreign Office Architects, *FOA's Arc: Phylogenesis* (Barcelona: Actar, 2002), 270–79.

NOTES

1. Demetri Porphyrios, *Sources of Modern Eclecticism: Studies on Alvar Aalto* (London: Academy Editions/St Martin's Press, 1982), 1.

2. See Michel Foucault, *The Order of Things. An Archaeology of the Human Sciences* (New York: Vintage Books, 1973), xviii.

3. 'Christian Norberg-Schulz: A Talk with Mies van der Rohe', published in *Baukunst und Werkform*, 11:11 (1958), 615–18, trans. Mark Jarzombek and rpt. in Fritz Neumeyer, *The Artless Word: Mies van der Rohe and the Building Art* (Cambridge, MA: MIT Press, 1991), 338–39.

4. Alison and Peter Smithson, *Without Rhetoric*, 19 and *Mies's Pieces*, 16, 33.

5. The event is recorded in the yearbook *Integral*, 1958 (Chicago: Students of the Illinois Institute of Technology, 1958), 106–07.

6. See Johann Wolfgang von Goethe, *The Metamorphosis of Plants*, trans. Agnes Arber, in *Chronica Botanica* 10:2 (Summer 1946).

7. Johann Wolfgang von Goethe, *The Metamorphosis of Plants*. trans. Anne E Marshall and Heinz Grotzke (Wyoming, Rhode Island: Bio-Dynamic Literature, 1978), 20.

MIES'S EVENT SPACE

When the New National Gallery (NNG) in Berlin opened on
15 September 1968, the critics celebrated it as a monumental
work by one of the greatest architects of the twentieth
century, a homecoming for Mies van der Rohe, who had left
for Chicago in 1938 and was now 82 years old, too frail to
attend the event. Yet almost immediately there were also
voices of dissent, critics who pointed to functional problems in displaying art in the great glass hall under the
levitated grid, a space that was colossal in scale, dwarfing
most paintings and sculpture, that was almost entirely
open, without walls for mounting art, and was enclosed
completely in glass, letting light and views stream in unless
the curtains were drawn. Notwithstanding the seriousness
of the concerns, the critics excused these functional difficulties in recognition of the architect's own artistic achievement. After all, the spirit of the commission had been first
and foremost to secure a representative late work by Mies
in Berlin and to worry about its function secondarily. Many
people *still* think that Mies was simply indifferent to his
clients' needs, indifferent to the needs of displaying art,
imposing on them a work of art to be valued as an end in
itself. Moreover, this was a work first conceived for a
different purpose and a different climate (the offices of
Bacardi in Santiago, Cuba), already once transported to
Germany and offered unsuccessfully for a gallery (the
Georg Schäfer Museum project in Schweinfurt), now
enlarged and transposed to another city and another
context. For later critics, the problems of functionality were
symptomatic of the problems of universalist ideology,
Mies's quest for a universal space overriding difference for
the sake of sameness and control.

Yet, the story of these difficulties is not that simple.

147

Mies knew full well what troubles he was creating for the curators, not through indifference, but precisely *because* he cared about art and, especially, it would seem, about the future of art. 'It is very difficult', he acknowledged, 'to do an exhibition there. No question. But a great possibility for new ways to do it. And I think that I would not want to miss that.'[1] For Mies, the task at hand in Berlin was not just to house the art of the past, the great collection of easel paintings and figurative sculpture, which was accommodated quite well, after all, in the permanent galleries and sculpture garden on the lower level,[2] but rather to support and even provoke the emergence of new ways of displaying and experiencing art, perhaps even new ways of making it.

This was certainly not the first time that Mies set his architecture in the service of new ways of living and, thereby, set it against the perpetuation of old habits and forms. In the 1920s, he spoke of providing 'a ground for the unfolding of life', while the artist Hans Richter called him a new kind of architect, a *Baumeister* for a time of transition, a catalyst and agent of historical change.[3] Theo van Doesburg, too, singled Mies out as a leader among the younger generation whose work was demonstrative of the future, enabling observers to experience it proleptically, in advance of its fuller realisation.[4]

The inaugural exhibition at the New National Gallery – a retrospective of Piet Mondrian – reveals something of the new paradigm in the arts that Mies believed was unfolding. Recognising that the paintings were too small to be shown effectively in the big glass hall, Mies designed a

View of opening of the inaugural exhibition, Mondrian, at the New National Gallery, Berlin, 1968

system of suspended wall-sized panels onto which the paintings were mounted. The open configuration of the panels created more intimate spaces for viewing the paintings without interrupting the continuity of the larger space. While critics admired the ingenuity of this solution, they nevertheless pointed to the problems inherent in displaying painting in the great hall and found it disconcerting to see the legs of visitors moving beneath the panels. The idea may have been inspired by exhibitions in Cullinan Hall, which Mies had designed for the Museum of Fine Arts in Houston in 1954–58: exhibitions curated by James Johnson Sweeney with paintings floating in mid-air without any architectural support at all. Mies himself had already envisioned something like this in a collage for the hypothetical Museum for a Small City (1942–43) in which a painting by Wassily Kandinsky hovers above the ground next to a sculpture by Aristide Maillol. Notwithstanding this image, however, it is rare to find levitated planes in Mies's work. While Mies, like Theo van Doesburg, took the plane to be a new fundamental element of modern architecture, he preferred the freestanding wall to the floating plane, affirming gravity and the ground while embracing the open plan and spatial continuum.

The most direct evidence of Mies's ideas about new ways of exhibiting art at the NNG is found in a model of 1964 showing a possible exhibition in which two very large wall-sized paintings, abstract expressionist in nature, stand as freestanding planes among the wood partitions and marble shafts of the building and, curiously, a tree. The

Office of Mies van der Rohe, New National Gallery, Berlin, model with hypothetical exhibition installation, 1964

image recalls a series of collages, beginning with the Court House projects of the 1930s, in which Mies gradually developed a distinctive idea about combining painting, sculpture, architecture and landscape. Some of the ethereal interior perspectives include rectangles of wood texture pasted onto the sheet to represent freestanding walls such as the ebony wall of the Tugendhat House with its optically charged grain.[5] Other collages incorporate fragments of a painting by Georges Braque, *Fruit Dish, Sheet Music and Pitcher* of 1926. By taking only a fragment of the Braque painting and inverting it,

Mies dissociated it from the actual work and transformed what was representational into a pure abstract composition of colour, enlarged to architectural scale and legible at a distance.

The well-known collage of the Resor House of 1939 combines a wood wall, a fragment of Paul Klee's painting *Bunte Mahlzeit* (Colourful Meal) of 1928 and a photograph of the landscape visible through the floor-to-ceiling panoramic windows – one instance each of an architectural element (the wall), a painting and a landscape, brought together in an assemblage. This marks a new kind of unity through montage, one that respects, even heightens, the integrity and autonomy of each work and each medium, while bringing them into a structural and proportional relationship to one another. This is not a *Gesamtkunstwerk* (total work of art) in which the operative principle is fusion, but rather an *Einheitskunst* (art of unity) in which a common principle (inner cause) is understood to underpin the different forms of artistic practice and the expression of their inner logic. Moreover, the collage foregrounds the elementary character and material facture of each, which at a certain level of abstraction begins to suggest structural, in other words organisational, affinities lurking within the surface of appearance.

In this respect, the three pieces of this collage share an affinity with the flattening and estranging photography of Albert Renger-Patzsch (for example *Beech Logs*, 1926), Umbo (for example *Mysteries of the Street*, 1928), László Moholy-Nagy (for example *Marseilles*, 1929) and others who, in the 1920s, developed a 'new objectivity' in photography, exploiting the capacity of the camera to reveal a world of secret truths and universal forms unavailable to the naked eye. As vice-president of the Deutscher Werkbund, Mies was well aware of the new objectivity and the new optics featured in the Werkbund's 'Film und Foto' exhibition of 1929, organised largely by Moholy-Nagy and commemorated in publications by Mies's friends Richter and Werner Graeff, as well as the historian/critic Franz Roh.

In the Resor House collage, the abstracting effect of

the close-up is most evident in the fragment of Klee's *Bunte Mahlzeit*, whereas in the collage of the *Museum for a Small City* of 1943 it is most evident in the photographs of the landscape – in the surface of water and the pattern of leaves – while the painting, in this case Picasso's *Guernica* of 1937, is shown in its totality. Despite this reversal, the abstracted figuration of the painting is in scale with the building and in proportion with the sculptures by Maillol and even the enlarged patterns of water and leaves beyond. Through careful relationships Mies created ensembles that enhanced the uniqueness, difference and individuality of elements and works while simultaneously bringing their underlying material organisation (elemental and atomic) into alignment and visibility.

The combination of autonomy and homology, difference and sameness is paradigmatic of Mies's conception of *Bildung* for people (formation, cultivation and learning) and *Gestaltung* for art, technology and buildings (the self-generated creation of form through elemental means, and individuation through inner cause). Mies understood autonomy not as an isolated *autopoiesis* but as a kind of self-fashioning that is embedded in and responsive to context. Individuation was understood to occur with structures – social structures, economic structures and structures of mind and of existence – but also to actualise these structures. For Mies, the capacity for *Bildung* had been lost with the great detachment of the individual from the community that began in the Renaissance and assumed gargantuan proportions with the advent of mass society in the late nineteenth and early twentieth centuries.[6] Renewing this capacity became increasingly key to his conception of the task at hand. If the architecture of the NNG – especially its gridded roof – is an essay in making implicit structure explicit and tangible, it also provides a setting for others to explore the same goal in different artistic media.

Mies's collages of the 1930s and 1940s belong to a history of avant-garde critiques of traditional forms of art which underpinned numerous experiments towards a new environmental paradigm intended to reunite the arts and reunite art with life. The abstract, colouristic and immersive environments envisioned in the 1920s by Bruno Taut, Theo van Doesburg, Kurt Schwitters, El Lissitzky and Le Corbusier are only the best known of these experiments. The Barcelona Pavilion (1928–29) demonstrated Mies's own version with a hybrid spatial structure – part *open plan* and part *free plan*. However, Mies rejected the application of coloured pigment to architectural surfaces and instead used colour only as an integral property of architectural materials. He made freestanding walls (as well as floors and ceilings) not of uniform hues but of uniform material: glass, wood, marble and plaster. Where El Lissitzky attempted to absorb small paintings and sculptural works into the overall composition of his *Abstract Cabinets* in Dresden (1926) and Hanover (1927–28), Mies understood, as did others of his generation, that framed paintings would ultimately be superseded by wall-sized works, contributing to a new unity of the arts within a new open and fluid spatiality. Having imagined such a possibility in the 1930s, it is hardly surprising that Mies responded as enthusiastically as he did to Picasso's *Guernica* when it appeared in Chicago in 1939-40 – at last, a wall-sized painting that demanded to become a freestanding wall in Mies's conception of the museum.

Reviewing the model of the NNG made in 1964 and the collages that preceded it helps to revivify what Mies might have understood the emerging paradigm of art to be. However, it would be hard to claim that this new unity of painting, sculpture, architecture and landscape was the only form of display that Mies anticipated for the gallery's exhibition hall. This space was, after all, intended for temporary exhibitions whose specific nature could not be predicted in advance. And it extends his exploration of the flexible open plan – the 'variable ground plan' or 'universal space' – that he had been developing since the early 1940s and whose primary virtue was the capacity to accommodate change. The openness of the long-span glass and steel pavilion constitutes another way in which the NNG supported new ways of displaying art, which comes into focus when we look at the history of exhibitions and events held there over the past 30 years.

Following the Mondrian show, the history of exhibitions at the New National Gallery reveals a diversity of responses to the building, some consistent with Mies's vision, some brilliant in unexpected ways, and others decidedly awkward. Although the curators found Mies's suspended panels too cumbersome in their size and weight (substantial equipment was required to move them around), they used them for several more shows, including an exhibition of large paintings by Roberto Sebastian Antonio Matta in 1970. In 1977, the exhibition of François Morrellet featured large paintings hung directly from the ceiling, harking back to Sweeney's shows at Cullinan Hall. As an alternative, however, an exhibition system of demountable wall panels with overhead structure and lighting track was commissioned in 1977 from designer Walter Kuhn of Hannover in order to facilitate variable configurations of more intimate spaces for smaller works. Although it also was an awkward means of displaying art and competed with the larger architectural frame, it was used for over seven years. Beginning in this period, but more consistently later on, extensive walls and even rooms were constructed directly on the floor within the great hall. Examples of this include the AR Penck exhibition of 1988 and 'Art Spaces – Visiting the National Gallery' (Kunsträume – Zu Gast in der Nationalgalerie) of 1987. In 1997 Frank O Gehry used this strategy to design an effective installation for 'Exiles and Emigres'.

In the 1970s the space began to be used for installation art as well as multi-media installations. Panamarenko's blimp was shown together with smaller inventions and wall-mounted works in 1978, and Mario Merz's *Drop of Water (Igloo)* of 1987 was featured in the show 'Positions in Contemporary Art'. The Douglas Gordon show in 1998 (featuring *5 Year Drive By* and *Bootleg (Empire)*) continued this genre, appearing to fulfil Mies's desire for large-scale works albeit now in the medium of video. For his show in

2000 the architect Renzo Piano created a richly layered installation of suspended horizontal vitrines punctuated with floating prototypes of roof elements and structural joints, revisiting the idea of suspension from the Mondrian show but without subdividing the great hall into smaller spaces: in this way he achieved a heightened sense of lightness, transparency and theatricality.

The space has also been used for performances, including the Metamusik Festival in 1974, the circus that was part of the exhibition 'Circus' in 1978, a performance by the La Mamma theatre, and Daniele Lombardi's *Symphony for 21 Pianos*. The installation of Alberto Giacometti's attenuated existential figures in 1988 also had something of the quality of a performance when seen in silhouette or in relation to visitors moving through the gallery.

More recently, there have been several solo exhibitions of site-specific work in which artists have actively engaged the architecture in dialogue. This is not a kind of work that Mies anticipated, although his building lends itself especially well to those that enter into its logic or respond – be it affirmatively or critically – to his desire to manifest the deep structure immanent in creation. While Matt Mullican's *Banners* of 1995 clearly belong to the building in their scale and proportion – their graphic language echoes the universalist ambitions of the building – they are at the same time entirely alien to it, blocking its transparency with sheets of bold, colourful icons that radically transform the image of the building outside and render the experience inside almost claustrophobic. More subtly, Ulrich Rückriem's installation of 1999–2000 placed stones that were exactly the size of the building module on the floor in a pattern generated through a locational formula that was both random and rigorous, thereby stretching the logic of the grid beyond the limit of pure rationality.

Where Rückriem occupied the floor, Jenny Holzer took over the ceiling with SMPK in 2001. By attaching lines of moving electronic text to the underside of Mies's dark artificial sky, Holzer transformed the grid's implied extension to the horizon on all sides into a one-way flow of information. Like soldiers marching in formation, row upon row of provocative yet enigmatic slogans rushed by overhead, at times very quickly or with the lights oscillating so that their messages could only be read a few words at a time, becoming abstract, a wave flowing through and beyond the grid.

Most recently, in 2003, the exhibition 'Content' by Rem Koolhaas and OMA took aim at the pristine purity of the glass box and filled it up with scattered detritus from the designs of their most recent buildings and urban projects – models and maquettes in different materials and scales, graphic presentations of research data and imagery, material studies, engineering calculations and even the media spectacle of global politics. If in Mies's time, the production of difference or events required emptiness, today, Koolhaas implies, it requires fullness of content, a cacophony of junk and flows of information and politics as much as matter.

The variety of shows and events held at the NNG, beginning with the *Richtfest* celebrating the raising of the roof, points to its function as a framework or infrastructure for an experimental approach to art and life in which the question of autonomy extends to the curators and artists themselves. It is something like a black box theatre, a flexible tool capable of being adapted to different functions and desires, not unlike Cedric Price's Fun Palace project of 1961–64 – a giant Erector Set in which British workers were to realise their 'potential for self-expression by dancing, beating drums, Method-acting, tuning in on Hong Kong in closed-circuit television and action painting'.[7] In this respect, the NNG also shows an affinity with Coop Himmelblau's *Large Cloud Scene* of 1976 – a temporary structure in Vienna, four framework towers 13 metres high with heaven stretched between them, an open setting for events, mobile performances, circuses and street-fests, hoping to increase the vitality of urban life in order to precipitate urban change.

As with Price's project, there is no set script for Mies's

stage, nor is there a teleology to be performed. Instead its
extreme openness anticipates dramatic events. Mies
captured this spirit in a sketch that is a diagram of life in
the universal space, the open yet lightly structured space
within which partitions, furniture and installations can be
configured and reconfigured with ease. With a few strokes
of his pencil, Mies marked the edges of a square box within
which a squiggly line circles around the empty centre, an
event whose form and character remain indeterminate.
The swirling flux has yet to settle or harden into forms or
striations, is still in the process of becoming, is smooth,
even chaotic, little more than a potential. Mies's squiggly
line depicts the potentiality of becoming, the potential to
actualise being in a multiplicity of contingent concrete
configurations over time. This is the spirit of Mies's quest
for the 'almost nothing' that takes us back to what, for
millennia, has been understood as the original nothingness
and potentiality of existence. Like Kasimir Malevich's *Black
Square* of 1915, it is all and nothing. If people are disturbed
and unsettled by its ascetic emptiness, that is precisely its
point: to create within the world – the world that is already
fixed in form – a clearing, a radical negation, an open space
that demands and facilitates the production of being, as
close to pure presence as possible. Mies's glass box is so
minimal, its infrastructure so well integrated and its
elements so reduced and simplified that it is little more
than a recessive, neutral and empty architectonic in which
to play at a modernity whose realisation is continually
deferred.

However, the palpable discomfort of many of the
installations in the NNG suggests that its architecture is
not, after all, the same as Price's more accommodating
Erector Set, or for that matter, the neutral white box that has
become paradigmatic of galleries for contemporary art.
While open to change and new ways of doing things, it is
not neutral after all. In Mies's phrase, it is *'almost* nothing',
and if we put the emphasis on the 'almost' rather than the
'nothing', then we realise that it *is* something in fact,
something material and tangible that operates between us

and nothing, that points to nothing, plays the role of nothing, allows us to imagine nothing and even experience its terror, keeping the chill of nothing at bay while harnessing its catalytic agency. The NNG is, in fact, a resolutely fixed and unchanging frame that is charged with symbolic, even metaphysical, implications, like the dome of a cathedral. And like a cathedral, the purpose of its analogy to the heavens is to take us outside ourselves, beyond the human – to contemplate and experience alterity without appropriating it. At the NNG, this extension occurs in the floor as well as the roof, as the building opens to and frames the plaza, the city and the horizon beyond. Mies did not offer technology as tool, empirical, functional and transparent. Instead he transformed technology into an architectonic image that was at once technological, artistic, historical and cosmological.

This image provides a stage – almost transparent – on which the homelessness and nihilism so central to the experience of modernity can be enacted as both a crisis *and* an opportunity for constructive self-fashioning. On this stage, some performances succeed better than others, while some fail miserably and are seen to do so. The more the exhibitions have pushed beyond the conventions of traditional art and engaged with the scale of the building and the problematics of modernity, the more successful they have been. Nor is the New National Gallery the same as Coop Himmelblau's temporary event structure. Mies's dark artificial sky is not only durable but enduring, heavy in both the literal and figurative sense of the word, less optimistic and light-hearted, more demanding but also galvanising in its evocation of the structure of existence.

Originally published in *Grey Room* 20 (2005), 60–73

MODERNITY UNBOUND

NOTES

1. See interview with Ludwig Mies van der Rohe in the film by Michael Blackwood, *Mies* (New York: Michael Blackwood Productions, 1987).

2. The formation of the Neue Nationalgalerie Berlin brought together the collections of the Nationalgalerie of the Stiftung Preussischer Kulturbesitz and the Twentieth Century Collection of the City of Berlin. The Nationalgalerie had been established in 1861 and became one of the greatest collections of post-1800 art. In 1937 the Nazis destroyed or sold nearly 500 works. More perished during WWII, and others were taken to the Soviet Union and only returned much later.

3. Richter, 'Der neue Baumeister', *Qualität* 4 (January/February 1925), 3–9.

4. Theo van Doesburg, 'The Dwelling: The Famous Werkbund Exhibition', trans. Charlotte I Loeb and Arthur L Loeb, *On European Architecture. Complete Essays from* Het Bouwbedriff, 1924–1931 (Basel: Birkhäuser, 1990), 164. Original essay published in *Het Bouwbedriff*, 4:24 (November 1927), 556–59.

5. I am indebted to Kenneth Hayes for his analysis of these collages and more generally for his insights into the shift from easel painting to wall-sized works and immersive environments.

6. Ludwig Mies van der Rohe, 'The Preconditions of Architectural Work', 1928, in Fritz Neumeyer, The Artless Word: Mies van der Rohe and the Building Art (Cambridge, MA: MIT Press, 1991), 301.

7. Ruth Langdon Inglis, 'Architecture: The Fun Palace', *Art in America*, 54 (January/February 1966), 69–72.

BIOCONSTRUCTIVISMS

On meeting the German structural engineer Frei Otto in 1997, Lars Spuybroek was struck by the extent to which Otto's approach to the design of light structures was resonant with his own interest in the generation of complex and dynamic curvatures. Having designed the Freshwater Pavilion (1994–97) through geometric and topological procedures, which were then materialised through a steel structure and flexible metal sheeting, Spuybroek found in Otto a reservoir of experiments in developing curved surfaces of even greater complexity through a process that was already material – that was, in fact, simultaneously material, structural and geometric. Moreover, Otto's concern with flexible surfaces not only blurred the classic distinctions between surface and support, vault and beam (suggesting a non-elemental conception of structural functions) but made construction and structure a function of movement, or more precisely a function of the rigidification of soft, dynamic entities into calcified structures such as bones and shells. Philosophically inclined toward a dynamic conception of the universe – a Bergsonian and Deleuzian ontology of movement, time and duration – Spuybroek embarked on an intensive study of Otto's work and took up his analogical design method. A materialist of the first order, Spuybroek now developed his own experiments following those of Otto with soap bubbles, chain nets and other materials as a way to discover how complex structural behaviours find forms on their own accord, which can then be reiterated on a larger scale using tensile, cable or shell constructions.

This curious encounter between Spuybroek and Otto sends us back not only to the 1960s but deeper in time. The recent re-engagement of architecture with generative models from nature, science and technology is itself part of a longer history of architects, engineers and theorists pursuing *autopoiesis* or self-generation. While its procedures and forms have varied, self-generation has been a consistent goal in architecture for over a century, set against the perpetuation of predetermined forms and norms. The well-known polemic of the early twentieth-century avant-garde against received styles or compositional systems in art and architecture – and against style *per se* – may, in fact, be understood as part of a longer and larger shift in thought from notions of predetermination to self-generation, from transcendence to immanence. The search for new methods of design has been integral to this shift, whether it be figured in terms of a period-setting revolution or the immanent production of multiplicity. Although a history of generative architecture has yet to be written, various partial histories in art, philosophy and science may serve to open this field of research.

In his landmark cross-disciplinary study, *Self-Generation: Biology, Philosophy and Literature around 1800* (1997), Helmut Müller-Sievers describes how the Aristotelian doctrine of the epigenesis of organisms – having been challenged in the seventeenth century by the rise of modern sciences – resurfaced in the eighteenth century, as the mechanistic theories of Galileo, Descartes and Newton floundered in their explanations of the appearance of new organisms. Whereas figures such as Charles Bonnet and Albrecht von Haller held that the germs of all living beings had been pre-formed since the Creation – denying nature any productive energy – a new theory of self-generation gradually took shape. An active inner principle was first proffered by Count Buffon and then elaborated by Caspar Friedrich Wolff, explaining the production of new organisms through the capacity of unorganised, fluid material to consolidate itself. Johann Friedrich Blumenbach transformed Wolff's 'essential force' into a 'formative drive' that served as the motive for the successive self-organisation of life forms, understanding this as a transition from unorganised matter to organised corporations.[1]

The biological theory of epigenesis came to underpin the theory of autonomy in the human sphere – in art, aesthetics, philosophy, politics and social institutions such as marriage. As Müller-Sievers has noted, Blumenbach's epigenesis provided a direct model for Kant's deduction of the categories, on which his shift from metaphysics to epistemology relied: 'Only if they are self-produced can the categories guarantee transcendental apriority and, by implication, cognitive necessity and universality'.[2]

In a similar vein, but looking to mathematics and its influence rather than biology or aesthetics, the philosopher David Lachterman characterised the whole of modernity as 'constructivist' and traced its origins further back to the shift in the seventeenth century from ancient to modern mathematics. Where the mathematics of Euclid focused on axiomatic methods of geometric demonstration and the proof of theorems (existence of beings), modern mathematics emphasised geometrical construction and problem-solving.[3] As Lachterman put it, a fairly direct line runs from the 'construction of a problem' in Descartes through the 'construction of an equation' in Leibniz to the 'construction of a concept' in Kant.

Rather than reiterating ontologies of sameness, modern mathematics sought to produce difference through new constructions. In this regard it is telling that, as Lachterman points out, Euclidean geometry arose against a platonic backdrop which understood each of the mathematicals as having unlimited manyness. According to the doctrine of intermediates, 'the mathematicals differ from the forms inasmuch as there are many 'similar' [*homoia*] squares, say, while there is only one unique form'. Lachterman continues,

The manyness intrinsic to each 'kind' of figure as well as the manyness displayed by the infinitely various images of each kind must somehow be a multiplicity indifferent to itself, a manyness of differences that make no fundamental difference, while nonetheless never collapsing into indiscriminate sameness or identity with one another.'[4]

A Euclidean construction, then, does not produce heterogeneity, but rather negotiates an intricate mutuality between manyness and kinship, variation and stability. It is always an image of this one, uniquely determinate, specimen of the kind. 'There is no one perfect square, but every square has to be perfect of its kind, not *sui generis*.'[5]

The quest for *autopoiesis* has been expressed, then, in a variety of oppositional tropes – creation versus imitation, symbol versus rhetoric, organism versus mechanism, epigenesis versus pre-formation, autonomy versus metaphysics and construction *sui generis* versus reiteration of Forms. In the nineteenth century, such binary oppositions came to underpin the quest for freedom among the cultural avant-garde. In his *Five Faces of Modernity* (1987), Matei Calinescu recounted that the term 'avant-garde' was first introduced in military discourse during the Middle Ages to refer to an advance guard. It was given its first figurative meaning in the Renaissance, but only became a metaphor for a self-consciously advanced position in politics, literature and art during the nineteenth century. In the 1860s, Charles Baudelaire was the first to point to the unresolved tension within the avant-garde between radical artistic freedom and programmatic political campaigns modelled on war and striving to install a new order – between critique, negation and destruction, on the one hand, and dogma, regulation and system, on the other. An alternative interpretation of what Calinescu calls the *aporia* of the avant-garde – one that sharpens the implications of this problematic, both philosophically and politically – is suggested by Michael Hardt and Tony Negri's account of the origins of modernity in their book, *Empire* (2000). Their history is even more sweeping than those reviewed above, summarising how, in Europe between 1200 and 1400, divine and transcendental authority over worldly affairs came to be challenged by affirmations of the powers of this world, which they call 'the [revolutionary] discovery of the plane of immanence.' Citing further evidence in the writings of Nicholas of Cusa among others, Hardt and Negri conclude that the primary event of modernity was constituted by shifting knowledge from the transcendental plane to the immanent, thereby turning knowledge into a doing, a practice of transforming nature. Galileo Galilei went so far as to suggest that it was possible for humanity to equal divine knowledge (and hence divine doing), referring specifically to the mathematical sciences of geometry and arithmetic. As Lachterman suggested using somewhat different terms, on the plane of immanence, mathematics begins to operate differently than it does within philosophies of transcendence where it secures the higher order of being. On the plane of immanence, mathematics is done constructively, solving problems and generating new entities. For Hardt and Negri, 'the powers of creation that had previously been consigned exclusively to the heavens are now brought down to earth.'

By the time of Spinoza, Hardt and Negri note, the horizon of immanence and the horizon of democratic political order had come together, bringing the politics of immanence to the fore as both the multitude, in theoretical terms, and a new democratic conception of liberation and of law through the assembly of citizens.[6] The historical process of subjectivisation launched an immanent constitutive power and with it a politics of difference and multiplicity. This in turn sparked counter-revolutions, marking the subsequent history as 'an uninterrupted conflict between the immanent, constructive, creative forces and the transcendent power aimed at restoring order.'[7] For Hardt and Negri, this crisis is constitutive of modernity itself. Just as immanence is never achieved, so the counter-revolution is also never assured.

The conflict between immanence and transcendence may also be discerned in architecture, along with efforts to resolve it through the mediation of an architectonic system for free expression or self-generation. Critical of using historical styles, which were understood as residual transcendent authorities no longer commensurate with the present, progressive architects of the early twentieth century sought to develop a modern style that, in itself, would also avoid the problem of predetermination, which

had taken on new urgency under the conditions of industrialisation and mass production. Such a style was conceived
more in terms of procedures than formal idioms. For
instance, in a piece of history that has received inadequate
attention, a number of Dutch architects around 1900 turned
to proportional and geometric constructions as generative
tools. Recognising that classical, but also medieval and
even Egyptian, architecture employed proportional
systems and geometric schema, they hoped to discover a
mathesis universalis, both timely and timeless, for a process
of design whose results were not already determined at the
outset. The validity and value of such forms were guaranteed, it was thought, by virtue of the laws of geometry,
whose own authority was in turn guaranteed by their
giveness in nature. Foremost among a group that included
JH de Groot, KPC de Bazel, PJH Cuypers and JLM Lauweriks, was HP Berlage, whose celebrated Stock Exchange in
Amsterdam (1901) was based on the Egyptian triangle.

In lectures and publications of around 1907 – synop-
ses of which were translated and published in America in
1912 – Berlage articulated his theory of architecture based
on the principles and laws of construction. Taking issue
with the growing pluralism of taste-styles, he sought an
objective basis for design – including the peculiarities of
construction and the arrangement of forms, lines and
colours – in the laws of nature. He described these as 'the
laws under which the Universe is formed, and is constantly
being reformed; it is the laws which fill us with admiration
for the harmony with which everything is organised, the
harmony which penetrates the infinite even to its invisible
atoms'.[8] He went on to argue that adherence to nature's
laws and procedures need not lead to mindless repetition
and sameness, since nature produces a boundless variety
of organisms and creatures through the repetition of basic
forms and elements. Similarly, he considered music a
paradigm, since here too creativity appeared unhampered
in the adherence to laws.

Citing Gottfried Semper, Berlage extended this
analogy to suggest that even evolution is based on 'a few

normal forms and types, derived from the most ancient traditions'. They appear in an endless variety that is not arbitrary but determined by the combination of circumstances and proportions, by which he meant relations or, more precisely, organisation. For Berlage, this led directly – for both practical and aesthetic reasons – to mathematics in art as in nature. He wrote:

I need only remind you in this connection of the stereometric-ellipsoid forms of the astral bodies, and of the purely geometrical shape of their courses; of the shapes of plants, flowers and different animals, with the setting of their component parts in purely geometrical figures; of the crystals with their purely stereometric forms, even so that some of their modification remind one especially of the forms of the Gothic style; and lastly, of the admirable systematism of the lower animal and vegetable orders, in latter times brought to our knowledge by the microscope, and which I have myself used as motif for the designs of a series of ornaments.[9]

It is worth noting that, as Berlage was putting forward a constructivist cosmology of architecture, Peter Behrens in Germany drew on some of the same proportional systems but with a more conservative agenda, reiterating the transcendent claims of classicism through a neo-Kantian schematism. For Behrens, geometry constituted an *a priori* architectonic system that was to be applied across buildings, landscapes and furniture to raise the material world to the higher plane of *Kultur*, while for Berlage a living geometry, in itself heterogeneous rather than homogeneous, was the basis for producing novel astylar forms that belonged to this world.[10] Behrens' pursuit of the 'great form' – symbol of the transcendence of pure mind and spirit – privileged architectonics over construction and maintained a clear hierarchy between the material and the ideal. For Berlage, by contrast, architecture was at once geometric, material, technological and biological. He understood beauty to be immanent to the self-actualisation of material entities, contingent only on the rational (*sachlich*) use of means and the laws of geometry.

In citing the 'admirable systematicalness of the lower animal and vegetable orders', Berlage alluded to the microscopic single-cell sea creatures studied by the German zoologist Ernst Haeckel in the 1880s and popularised in his book of 1904, *Kunstformen der Natur* (The Art Forms of Nature), as well as other writings, including his *Report of the Scientific Results of the Voyage of HMS Challenger* (London, 1887). Haeckel

Ernst Haeckel, *Kunstformen der Natur* (1904)

estimated that there were 4,314 species of radiolarians included in 739 genera found all over the world, without any evident limitations of geographical habitat.[11] He also noted that the families and even genera appear to have been constant since the Cambrian age. This unicellular species of organisms became an exemplar for those interested in learning from how self-generation in nature could produce seemingly endless variety – if not multiplicity *per se* – in complex as well as simple forms of life. Haeckel hoped that knowledge of ur-animals (protozoa such as radiolarians, thalamophora and infusorians) and ur-plants (protophntoa such as diatoms, rosmarians and veridienians) 'would open up a rich source of motifs for painters and architects' and that 'the real art forms of Nature not only stimulate the development of the decorative arts in practical terms but also raise the understanding of the plastic arts to a higher theoretical level.'[12]

In his own landmark book, *On Growth and Form* (1917), the Scottish biologist D'Arcy Wentworth Thompson developed science's understanding of form in terms of the dynamics of living organisms, their transformation through growth and movement.[13] In considering the formation of skeletons, he recounted Haeckel's theory of 'bio-crystallisation' among very simple organisms, including radiolarians and sponges. While the sponge-spicule offered a simple case of growth along a linear axis – the skeleton always beginning as a loose mass of isolated spicules – the radiolarian provided a more complex case among single-cell organisms, exhibiting extraordinary intricacy, delicacy and complexity as well as beauty and variety, all by virtue of the 'intrinsic form of its elementary constituents or the geometric symmetry with which these are interconnected and arranged.'[14] For Thompson, such 'biocrystals' represented something 'midway between an inorganic crystal and an organic secretion.'[15] He distinguished their multitudinous variety from that of snowflakes, which were produced through symmetrical repetitions of one simple crystalline form, 'a beautiful illustration of Plato's *One among the Many*.'[16] The generation of the radiolarian skeleton, on the other hand, is more complex and open-ended, for it 'rings its endless changes on combinations of certain facets, corners and edges within a filmy and bubbly mass'. With this more heterogeneous technology, the radiolarian can generate continuous skeletons of netted mesh or perforated lacework that are more variegated, modulated and intricate – even irregular – than any snowflake.[17]

For enthusiasts of biocrystallisation, one of the key features of the radiolarians was the apparently perfect regularity of their form, or more precisely of their skeleton and the outer surface layer of froth-like vesicles, 'uniform in size or nearly so', which tended to produce a honeycomb or regular meshwork of hexagons. The larger implications of this regularity were made explicit in scientific cosmologies of the early twentieth century, such as Emmerich Zederbauer's *Die Harmonie im Weltall in der Natur und Kunst* (1917) and Ernst Mössel's *Vom Geheimnis der Form und der Urform des Seines* (1938). Supported by the evidence of ever more powerful microscopes and telescopes, these authors sought to confirm that the entire universe was ordered according to the same crystalline structural laws – establishing continuity from the structure of molecules and microscopic radiolarians to macroscopic celestial configurations, between the organic and the inorganic, nature and technology.

Perhaps the most sweeping statement of platonic oneness at mid-century – embracing industrialised structures as well as natural ones – was provided by R Buckminster Fuller when he wrote that the 'subvisible microscopic animal structures called *radiolaria* are developed by the same mathematical and structural laws as those governing the man-designed geodesic and other non-man-designed spheriodal structures in nature.'[18] This similarity of underlying laws gave the radiolarians, like the geodesic domes that Fuller designed, the character of an exemplar for fundamental structures, which, he explained, were not in fact things but rather 'patterns of inherently regenerative constellar association of energy events'.[19] As if to substantiate Fuller's point, Paul Weidlinger illustrated his own account of isomorphism in organic and inorganic materials, as well as microscopic and macroscopic events, by comparing Haeckel's drawing of a radiolarian with a magnified photograph of soap bubbles, the stellate cells of a reed and one of Fuller's geodesic domes, replete with tiny spikes that reinforce its resemblance to the radiolarian.[20]

Yet Thompson's lengthy effort to account for the diversity of the tiny creatures ultimately ran aground on the impossible mathematics of Haeckel's theory of bio-crystallisation. Not only did Thompson find it necessary to acknowledge and examine less perfectly configured specimens, such as the *reticulum plasmatique* depicted by Carnoy, but in comparing them with Haeckel's *Aulonia* – 'looking like the finest imaginable Chinese ivory ball' – he invoked Euler to explain that 'No system of hexagons can enclose space; whether the hexagons be equal or unequal, regular or irregular, it is still under all circumstances mathematically impossible … the array of hexagons may be extended as far as you please, and over a surface either plane or curved, but it never closes in.'[21] Thompson pointed out that Haeckel himself must have been aware of the problem for, in his brief description of the *Aulonia hexagona*, he noted that a few square or pentagonal facets appeared among the hexagons. From this Thompson concluded that,

Two radiolarians, the *Reticulum plasmatique*, after Carnoy, and the *Aulonia hexagona*, as depicted by Ernst Haeckel

while Haeckel tried hard to discover and reveal the symmetry of crystallisation in radiolarians and other organisms, his effort 'resolves itself into remote analogies from which no conclusions can be drawn'. In the case of the radiolarians, 'Nature keeps some of her secrets longer than others.'[22]

During the 1960s, armed with evidence from advanced microscopes that the surface meshworks of radiolarians were in fact irregular, Phillip Ritterbush underscored the problem of regularity and biaxial symmetry when he suggested that Haeckel had altered his drawings of the radiolarians 'in order for them to conform more precisely to his belief in the geometric character of organisms'.[23] Ritterbush pointed out that Haeckel's appreciation of the regularities and symmetries of the skeletons of living organisms – and, by extension, Fuller's conception of geodesic domes as manifesting patterns of 'constellar' associations – relied on a permutation of the analogy with the crystal, which had been employed in biology since the seventeenth century. Nehemiah Grew (1628–1712), for instance, was an early plant anatomist who regarded regularities in natural forms as evidence that the processes of growth consisted of the repetition of simple steps, in which forms might be successfully analysed.

Fuller assumed that the modular regularity of the radiolarians demonstrated the existence of a universal transcendental order, and so reiterated it in the combinatorial logic of irreducible struts and universal joints that comprised his geodesic domes. In contrast, the botanist and popular science writer, Raoul H Francé, had already in the 1920s interpreted the radiolarians within a cosmology of composite assemblages that understood all of creation to be constructed not of one ur-element but of seven. In his *Die Pflanze als Erfinder* (The Plant as Inventor, 1920) Francé argued that the crystal, sphere, plane, rod, ribbon, screw and cone were the seven fundamental technical forms employed 'in various combinations by all world-processes, including architecture, machine elements, crystallography, chemistry, geography, astronomy and art – every technique in the world'. Comparing what he called the 'biotechnics' of maple keys and tiny flagellates moving through rotation with ships' propellers underscored the isomorphism between human and natural works, inspiring the Russian artist-architect El Lissitzky to denounce the fixation with machines in the early 1920s in favour of constructing 'limbs of nature'.[24] Francé was read enthusiastically in the mid-1920s by artists and architects who we associate with 'international constructivism' – not only El Lissitzky, but also Raoul Hausmann, László Moholy-Nagy, Hannes Meyer, Siegfried Ebeling and Ludwig Mies van der Rohe. So extensive was this reception of biotechnics or 'cosmobiotechnics', as Hausmann put it, that we may well refer to this orientation within constructivism as 'bioconstructivist'. Looking back, we may also recognise Berlage as providing an earlier iteration of bioconstructivist theory.

Lissitzky paraphrased Francé in his 'Nasci' issue of Merz in 1924, which he co-edited with Kurt Schwitters. It was there that Lissitzky gave a constructivist – and now scientific – twist to the idea of becoming that had saturated the Weimar artistic culture, associated with both Expressionism and Dada. The word *nasci* is Latin for 'begin life' and approximates *Gestaltung*, which was used in technical discourse as well as aesthetics and biology and referred simultaneously to form and the process of formation. It implied a self-generating process of form-creation through which inner purposes or designs became visible in outer shapes. Having reiterated Francé's theory of biotechnics in their introduction to the journal, Lissitzky and Schwitters then provided a portfolio of modern artworks that can only be interpreted as demonstrations of the theory. What is remarkable in this collection is the diversity produced with the seven technical forms. Beginning with Kasimir Malevich's *Black Square*, the folio then features one of Lissitzky's own Prouns; additional paintings by Piet

Mondrian and Fernand Léger; collages by Schwitters, Hans Arp and Georges Braque; sculpture by Alexander Archipenko; photograms by Man Ray; architecture by Vladimir Tatlin, JJP Oud and Ludwig Mies van der Rohe; and several phenomena from nature. The sequence concludes with an unidentified microscopic image punctuated by a question mark, suggesting something of the formlessness from which all form emerges or, perhaps, to which biotechnics might lead.

By the 1960s, scientists sought to come to terms with the limitations of the crystal metaphor for living phenomena. While Kathleen Lonsdale, for instance, attempted to shore up the transcendental authority of the crystalline by defining it more broadly as arrangements of atoms in repeating patterns,[25] the animal geneticist Conrad Waddington turned to other concepts to account for irregularities. Waddington used radiolarians to discuss not the similarities between organic forms and technological objects but the difference between them, characterising man-made objects as reductive, simplistic and monofunctional in comparison with the complex, varied and multipurpose nature of living organisms. For him, organic form 'is produced by the interaction of numerous forces which are balanced against one another in a near-equilibrium that has the character not of a precisely definable pattern but rather of a slightly fluid one, a rhythm'.[26] Invoking Alfred North Whitehead's conception of rhythm to address the irregularities with which Thompson had already struggled, Waddington wrote:

It is instructive to compare the character of the variations from the ideal form in an organic and in human creation. The shell of the minute unicellular organism *Aulonia hexagona* is one of those animal structures whose functions are simple enough for it to approximate to a simple mathematical figure, that of a sphere covered by almost regular hexagons. It will be seen that the hexagons are in practice not quite regular; they do not make up a rigidly definable pattern, but rather a rhythm, in the sense

of Whitehead, who wrote: 'A rhythm involves a pattern, and to that extent is always self-identical. But no rhythm can be a mere pattern; for the rhythmic quality depends equally upon the differences involved in each exhibition of the pattern. The essence of rhythm is the fusion of sameness and novelty; so that the whole never loses the essential unity of the pattern, while the parts exhibit the contrast arising from the novelty of the detail. A mere recurrence kills rhythm as surely as does a mere confusion of detail.'[27]

Like Waddington, the French-American structural engineer Robert le Ricolais – a pioneer of the space frame – insisted on distinguishing natural and man-made objects and on the limits of instrumental knowledge. While 'amazed' by the coherence and purity of design that the radiolarians represented, he also characterised it as 'frightening'. 'What man makes', he wrote, 'is usually single-purposed, whereas nature is capable of fulfilling many requirements, not always clear to our mind'.[28] Where engineers had been speaking about space frames for only 25 or 30 years, the radiolarians were, he explained, three hundred million years old. 'Well, it's not by chance, and I'm glad that I saw the Radiolaria before I saw Mr Fuller's dome.' Acknowledging that analogies with natural phenomena could help resolve some problems, he held that 'it's not so important to arrive at a particular solution as it is to get some general view of the whole damn thing, which leaves you guessing.'[29] Ricolais' use of material experiments was consistent with such scepticism, privileging specificity and concreteness over universal *mathesis*. Fascinated by the 'fantastic vastitude' of the radiolarians, neither Ricolais nor Frei Otto treated them as synecdoches for the entire universe.[30] They were merely one among many phenomena from which an engineer could learn.

During this period Frei Otto also took up the notion of self-generation and the analogy between biology and building, but eschewed the imitation of nature in favour of working directly in materials to produce models that were at once natural and artificial. At the same time, he also eschewed their translation into a universalising *mathesis*. Rather than focusing on form or formula, he took the idea of analogy in an entirely different direction, preferring to stage experiments in which materials find their own form. Where the theory of *Gestaltung* in the 1920s posited the unfolding of an essential germ from within, understanding external form as an expression of inner purpose, in the 1960s autogenesis was redefined through cybernetics and systems theory as a function of dynamic, open systems of organisation and patterning. In this context, Otto's experiments in the form-finding potential of material process sidestep purist essentialism to open up a world in which unique and complex structures result immanently from material exigencies without being subject to any transcendent authority, either internal or external. Otto's analogical models involve iterations on different scales and in different materials, but without positing an overarching totality, reductive universality or optimised homogeneity. Open to the air, rambling and polycentric, Otto's tensile structures operate demonstrably outside the terms of physiognomic and formal expression, leaving behind the problematics of inner–outer identity, closure and unity that had been integral to the modernist conception of the autonomous organism and of *autopoiesis* in human works.

It is telling that an entire issue of the *IL* journal of Otto's Institute for Lightweight Structures was devoted to radiolarians, whose composite of pneumatic and net structures intrigued Otto and his research group just as they did Ricolais. Unlike other admirers, however, Otto's group did not take these creatures as models for engineering, but rather sought to explain their self-generation with analogical models. Situated between natural phenomena and engineering, the isomorphic character of Otto's analogical models gives them not only instrumental value for new constructions but also explanatory power for natural phenomena.[31]

Spuybroek too is fascinated by how complex surfaces in nature result from the rigidification of flexible structures, a process so intricate as to elude precise theoretical or mathematical analysis. Like Otto, he uses a varied repertoire of analogical material models that are deceptively simple but remarkably effective for generating complex structures and tectonic surfaces. In his hands, radiolarians are no longer emblems of universal order, their imperfections corrected into the perfect regularity of crystalline spheres. 'What is so interesting about radiolarians', he writes, 'is that they are never spheres, though they tend towards the spherical. They are all composite spheres – tetrahedral, tubular, fan-shaped, etc.' Focusing on examples different from the perfect spheres singled out by Fuller, Spuybroek sees radiolarians not as homogeneous forms but as material technologies that produce hybrid tectonic surfaces – part pneumatic, part net structures – which are flexible in contour and shape. The rhythmic variability of these surfaces is achieved by changes in the size of openings and the thickness of the net fibres between them. With this shift from form to surface, Spuybroek leaves behind the modernist quest for the supposed self-same identity of the organism in favour of a surface that can be modulated to assume different shapes and sizes as well as various architectural roles – from facades to roofs and from towers to vaults, halls and edges. While Spuybroek's bundle of interwoven towers for the World Trade Center in New York demonstrates the flexibility of radiolarian technology, the more recent project for the European Central Bank realises its potential to operate simultaneously in a multitude of ways. More importantly still, Spuybroek's radiolarian tectonic surface is but one of an increasing repertoire of analogical models with which he works. Like Berlage and Francé, his organon of techniques is heterogeneous and divergent rather than homogeneous and convergent. Unlike them, however, he is no longer concerned with the elemental in any way, nor with unifying underlying laws, be they mathematical or biological or both. Although he employs the radiolarian technology to achieve what he calls 'a strong expression of wholeness and pluriformity at the same time,' his ECB is radically asymmetrical and irregular, polycentric and contingent. And while its pattern-structure implies repetition and extension, the buildings produced with it remain singular entities.

In taking over Otto's method, Spuybroek uses it as an abstract machine, understanding this term – and the broader pragmatics of which it is a part – through Gilles Deleuze and Felix Guattari.[32] In discussing regimes of signs in *A Thousand Plateaus* (1987), Deleuze and Guattari isolate four components of pragmatics: the generative, the transformational, the abstract machine, and the machinic. The generative, they say, 'shows how the various abstract regimes form concrete mixed semiotics, with what variants, how they combine, and which one is predominant'.[33] The transformational component, on the other hand, 'shows how these regimes of signs are translated into each other, especially when there is a creation of a new regime'.[34] However, they foreground the abstract machine, with its diagrammatic mode of operation, since it deterritorialises already established semiotic formations or assemblages, is 'independent of the forms and substances, expressions and contents it will distribute'[35] and plays a 'piloting role' in the construction of new realities. The machinic component, they conclude, shows 'how abstract machines are effectuated in concrete assemblages'.[36]

While their understanding of the generative is recombinatory and thus avoids implications of beginning from nothing, rethinking the generative impulse of the historical avant-garde in terms of the abstract machine helps to discharge any residual transcendentalism that continues to attend narratives of self-generation, which appears so anachronistic when reiterated by architects today. It offers a stronger and sharper version of *Gestaltung*, detaching process now entirely from form and dynamic organisation from *Gestalt*. Alternatively, we could say, with Zeynep Mennan, that it could lead to a *Gestalt*-switch, a new theory of *Gestalt* that would be adequate to complex, rhythmic and modulated forms of heterogeneity.[37] Rather than settling chaos into an order that presumes to transcend it, Spuybroek generates an architecture that is self-estranging and self-different, in which identity is hybrid, multiple and open-ended. If cosmological whole-ness is an issue at all, it may now be assumed as given, no longer something lost and needing to be regained, as the romantics thought. Art need no longer dedicate itself to the production of wholeness, since it is inherently part of the cosmos, whatever limited understanding of it we humans may achieve. As Keller Easterling has argued in another context, we need no longer worry about the One, but only the many.[38] There is no need for closure, unity or a system that assimilates everything into One.

Extending the bioconstructivism of Berlage, Francé, Lissitzky and Otto, Spuybroek now engages only in endless experiments with materials, their processes and structural potentials. What he repeats are not entities or forms but techniques, developing a new modus operandi for acting constructively in the world. Rather than seeking to over-come the world or to assimilate difference to the sameness of underlying laws, he works to produce new iterations of reality, drawing on the potentials of matter for the ongoing production and enjoyment of heterogeneous events.

Originally published in Lars Spuybroek, *NOX: Machining Architecture* (London: Thames & Hudson, 2004), 360–69.

NOTES

1. See Helmut Müller-Sievers, *Self-Generation: Biology, Philosophy and Literature around 1800* (Stanford: Stanford University Press, 1997).
2. Ibid., 46.
3. David Rapport Lachterman, *The Ethics of Geometry: A Genealogy of Modernity* (New York and London: Routledge, 1989), vii.
4. Ibid., 117-18.
5. Ibid., 118.
6. Michael Hardt and Antonio Negri, *Empire* (Cambridge, MA: Harvard University Press, 2000), 73.
7. Ibid., 77.
8. HP Berlage, 'Foundations and Development of Architecture (Part I)', *The Western Architect*, 18:9 (September 1912): 96-99; quotation is on page 96. Part 2 appears in 18:10 (October 1912): 104-108. These articles were based on his *Grundlagen der Architektur* (Berlin: Julius Bard, 1908), a series of five illustrated lectures delivered at the Kunstgewerbe Museum in Zurich in 1907.
9. Berlage, 'Foundations', part I, 97.
10. Berlage, *Grundlagen der Architektur*, 7, 16, 38-39.
11. Ernst Haeckel, *Report of the deep-sea Keratosa [collected by HMS Challenger during the years 1873-76]* (London: Eyre & Spottiswoode, 1889), clxxxviii.
12. Haeckel, *Kunstformen der Natur* (Leipzig and Vienna: Verlag des Bibliographischen Instituts, 1904), unpaginated introduction, translation by author.
13. D'Arcy Wentworth Thompson, *On Growth and Form* (New York: Dover, 1992). Originally published in 1917 and revised in 1942.
14. Ibid., 645.
15. Ibid., 691.
16. Ibid., 695.
17. Ibid., 698.
18. R Buckminster Fuller, 'Conceptuality of Fundamental Structures', in György Képes, ed., *Structure in Art and in Science* (New York: George Braziller, 1965), 66-88. The quotation is on 80.
19. Ibid., 66.
20. Paul Weidlinger, 'Form in Engineering' in György Képes, ed., *The New Landscape in Art and Science* (Chicago: Paul Theobald, 1956), 360-65.
21. Thompson, 708.
22. Ibid., 732.
23. Phillip Ritterbush, *The Art of Organic Forms* (Washington: Smithsonian Institution Press, 1968), 8. See also Donna Jeanne Haraway, *Crystals, Fabrics, and Fields: Metaphors of Organicism in Twentieth-Century Developmental Biology* (New Haven and London: Yale University Press, 1976), 11.
24. El Lissitzky and Kurt Schwitters, eds., 'Nasci', *Merz* 8/9 (April/July 1924). See translation of text in Sophie Lissitzky-Küppers, *El Lissitzky: Life, Letters, Works* (London: Thames & Hudson, 1992), 351.
25. Kathleen Lonsdale, 'Art in Crystallography', in György Képes, *The New Landscape in Art and Science* (Chicago: Paul Theobald, 1956), 358.
26. CH Waddington, 'The Character of Biological Form', in Lancelot Law Whyte, ed., *Aspects of Form* (London: Lund Humphries, 1951, 1968), 43-52.
27. Ibid., 26. Waddington's citation is from Alfred North Whitehead, *The Principles of Natural Knowledge* (Cambridge 1925), 198.
28. Interview with Robert Le Ricolais, 'Things themselves are lying, and so are their images', *VIA 2: Structures: Implicit and Explicit* (University of Pennsylvania, 1973), 91.

29. Ibid.
30. Ricolais used the term 'vastitude' in describing the variety of radiolarians.
31. The 1990 issue of the journal of the Institute for Lightweight Structures, *IL* 33, was dedicated to explaining the self-generation process in the skeletons of some radiolarians.
32. Gilles Deleuze and Félix Guattari, *A Thousand Plateaus: Capitalism and Schizophrenia*, translation and foreword by Brian Massumi (Minneapolis: University of Minnesota Press, 1987).
33. Ibid., 139.
34. Ibid.
35. Ibid., 141.
36. Ibid., 146.
37. Zeynep Mennan, 'Des formes non standard: un "Gestalt Switch"', in *Architectures non standard* (Paris: Centre Pompidou, 2003), 34-41.
38. Keller Easterling presented this argument in a lecture at the University of Pennsylvania on 19 November, 2003. See her book, *Enduring Innocence. Global Architecture and its Political Masquerades* (Cambridge, MA: MIT Press, 2005).

PERVASIVE PLASTICITY

The material we call 'concrete' is remarkable not only in the plasticity of the forms it can take but equally in its mutability and ever-increasing ubiquity. The last session of the Solid States conference, held at Columbia in the fall of 2008, addressed concrete's role in the unprecedented scale of global building production, while other discussions reported on current technical innovations and the new formal and spatial opportunities that they open up. Isn't it telling that concrete turns out to be as malleable technically as it is formally? And that much of today's innovation is driven by environmental issues that have become urgent, given the material's pervasive use: reducing carbon dioxide emissions, even sucking it out of the air and expanding the recycling of it. What I would like to do here is consider, through the lens of history – and admittedly with an orientation more formal than chemical – what happens when plasticity becomes normative?

In his landmark book *Building in France – Building in Iron – Building in Ferroconcrete* (1928), the historian Sigfried Giedion provided vivid evidence that iron construction had been the locus of great engineering in the nineteenth century but was superseded in the early twentieth by reinforced concrete.[1] He pointed to Le Corbusier's work on standardised housing to suggest that it would be through concrete rather than steel that the new spatial paradigm of modernity would be widely generalised. If Le Corbusier's Dom-ino (1914–15) captured this potential in a diagram, public housing programmes in Germany demonstrated its realisation at the urban scale, linking the modernisation of technology with the reconstruction of urban territories, albeit without Le Corbusier's internal spatial complexity. For the public housing programme in Frankfurt during the late 1920s, Ernst May ramped up the technology of precast concrete to build some 15,000 units of workers' housing in five years, in new garden settlements on the city's periphery. Achievements like this were formidable for the time and commensurate with the emergence of mass society, yet they pale in comparison with the scale and speed of urban growth in China today.

China's use of concrete in recent years has become the stuff of legend, accounting for half the world's total production and continuing to grow five per cent annually: in 2008 alone, some 5.5 million units of housing were realised in concrete. If we can say that Le Corbusier's Dom-ino concept now rules the day, it is not only because of the efficiency with which such structures can be produced – the radical reduction in material, time and labour they achieve, along with a radical expansion of scale – but also the flexibility with which this constructive system can adapt to different sites, scales, programmes, configurations, tastes and cultural desires. While appearing to delineate a rigid rationality, the Dom-ino system in fact possesses a plastic logic of variation and adaptation. The abandoned construction sites for hotels on the Sinai Peninsula, documented by Sabine Haubitz and Stefanie Zoche, illustrate how easily the Dom-ino system has incorporated non-Western cultural motifs, producing the kind of kitsch that has always been part of modernity. It is a system that mutates so easily that it often disconcerts the purists, exchanging Le Corbusier's cylindrical *pilotis* for piers, shear walls or other kinds of elements, and producing results that are structurally hybrid, like most commercial buildings or the more extreme 'turbo architecture' of Serbia.[2]

During the twentieth century concrete was typically celebrated, not for its systematic applications, but for enabling the realisation of unique sculptural forms – expressionist, biomorphic fantasies of a post-symbolist, post-art nouveau, post-futurist world to come, which would supersede and correct mechanisation. So strong was the desire for formal plasticity, complexity and alterity in the cultural imagination – for the organic, libidinal, Dionysian, delirious and dark – that concrete acquired a second material logic, directly at odds with its rationalist Dom-ino superego and the modernist ethos of honest construction. In 1919, for instance, when concrete was still in scarce supply after World War I, Erich Mendelsohn's Einstein Tower in Potsdam (1919–21) appeared to be made of concrete, when it was built in brick and merely pargeted with cement.

A few years later the theosophist, educator and designer Rudolf Steiner did use cast in-situ concrete for his Second Goetheanum in Dornach, Switzerland (1928), a building that remains inadequately recognised. It was immediately criticised and suppressed – together with other manifestations of apparent irrationality and Gothic desire – by so-called rationalists such as Giedion and Walter Gropius, who advocated a moralising embrace of industrial standardisation, although Giedion himself flirted with surrealism, as did his friend Le Corbusier.

Steiner had been a scholar of the writings of Johann Wolfgang von Goethe and sought to demonstrate a design approach based on natural principles identified in Goethe's new science of plant morphology (1790) – principles of form-generation and growth through an internal mechanism whose operation was not yet fully understood.[3] Taking up the question of what natural and artistic beauty might share in common, Goethe launched a search for laws of generation and development that were common to the works of nature and humanity. Goethe was a monist, which means that he saw the human as necessarily part of nature, a principle that underlies today's theories of deep ecology. In a similar though more idealist spirit, Karl Friedrich Schinkel had considered architecture the continuation by man of the constructive activity of nature.

In the same year that Steiner's Second Goetheanum opened (1928), Ludwig Karl Hilberseimer and Julius Vischer published a book on concrete entitled *Beton als Gestalter* (Concrete as Form-Creator).[4] As one might expect from Hilberseimer, it featured many examples of industrial buildings with column grids and expressed structural frames, but also domes such as Max Berg's powerful and pioneering Centennial Hall in Breslau (present-day Wroclaw, Poland) of 1911–13; long-span structures such as Erich Mendelsohn's Hat Factory in Luckenwalde, Germany (1919–20); and vaults such as Bruno Taut's exhibition hall in Magdeburg, the market hall in Reims and the aeroplane hangar by Eugène Freyssinet under construction in Orly, France, which was widely admired at the time.

Hilberseimer pointed out that the first patent for reinforced concrete had been filed in 1867 by the Parisian gardener Joseph Monier, who had used it to make vessels such as garden pots and large tubs. While Hilberseimer dismissed expressionist plasticity as arbitrary just as sternly as he rebuked historicist cladding of concrete skeletons, he commended the disciplined plasticity of cooling towers for following the laws of regularity, functionality and efficiency of means, and for a structural integrity that was also attributed to nature.

In the 1970s the historian Manfredo Tafuri character-ised this schism within the avant-garde in terms of a dialec-tic between rigourism and expressionism: Hannes Meyer's League of Nations (1927) versus Fritz Hoeger's Chilehaus in Hamburg (1924); and Gropius's Bauhaus at Dessau (1925–26) versus Erich Mendelsohn's Schocken department store in Chemnitz (1927–30).[5] He related this opposition of forms to what Theodor Adorno and Max Horkheimer had called the dialectic of Enlightenment in their 1940s analysis of cultural production under capitalism. It was the great insight of these critical theorists to recognise that the Enlightenment objective of banishing myth and superstition – regrounding knowledge and society strictly in reason and science – entailed the unacknowledged construction of new myths. Rather than vanquishing irrationality, Enlightenment thought was in fact shot through with myths, dark sides and violence. Rationality and myth turned out to be flip sides of the same coin, linked in an economy of repression and false consciousness.

But was this transposition of critical theory into

formal terms in fact warranted? Weren't both sides of the antagonism between Apollonian and Dionysian form equally enmeshed in the dialectic of Enlightenment? Did they not both manifest reason *and* myth at the same time? While expressionists emphasised the process of form-generation, functionalists also pursued organic principles as the way to supersede mechanistic rationality, although filtered through engineering. Few in architecture followed Freud's search for an understanding of the interplay between conscious and unconscious, ego and id, waking and dreaming.

Strangely, the antagonism of formal systems continues to structure architectural discussion today and is registered in competing approaches to concrete. On the one hand Kazuyo Sejima and Ryue Nishizawa continue to employ the Dom-ino system, usually with simple or slightly inflected geometries in plan, pushing its material logic to extremes of thinness and transparency. Many other firms, large and small, use concrete planes, columns and tubes in the spirit of the modern tradition that Giedion promoted at mid-century as a new vernacular for industrial society. On the other hand Zaha Hadid and many others – among them Coop Himmelb(l)au, Toyo Ito, UN Studio, Asymptote, Daniel Libeskind and Santiago Calatrava – treat concrete as an inherently plastic material to be shaped at will, like clay, into forms that are irregular, complex and often hybrid. New computational tools have made their work more easily mathematised, buildable, affordable and increasingly pervasive. Leveraging celebrity fame and the globalisation of practice, many of these firms have likewise grown to corporate scale, seeking to become at least as pervasive as the rigourists.

As this kind of experimental and highly individuated work enters mainstream development, mutations are emerging with ever-greater frequency. Frank Gehry's InterActiveCorp (IAC) building in New York (2007) is structured not with concrete shells, but with rather minor inflections of the Dom-ino system's orthogonal frame, relying on shaped glass to produce its complex, wave-like forms. Tall buildings – such as the Infinity Tower in Abu Dhabi by Skidmore, Owings & Merrill (SOM) – have become a favourite vehicle for architects to experiment with mutating normative structural systems to achieve plastic expressiveness.

In a recent essay in his book *Liquid Stone: New Architecture in Concrete*, Jean-Louis Cohen outlines a host of dichotomies that concrete has both sponsored and participated in. Expanding on the notion that both rigourists and expressionists have employed organic analogies, he writes:

The first model (Perret's rationalist cage) used finite vertical and horizontal elements assembled to produce a rigid concrete frame that evoked animal skeletons or vegetal stems. The second model (Niemeyer's lyrical shells) used continuous single- or double-curvature surfaces to produce thin vaults that evoked shells or membranes.[6]

Cohen calls the opposition between these systems simplistic and commends instead the hybridisation pioneered by Perret, in collaboration with his brother Gustav, in their Notre-Dame du Raincy church (1922–23), with its columnar, grid-and-shell roof. Of course, many more hybrids of this kind could be identified – just think of the work of the Manichean Le Corbusier – but is it possible to go beyond dualisms altogether?

Certainly that is one of the promises of parametric design, which has become so central to design research in recent years that Patrik Schumacher delivered a manifesto for parametricism at the Dark Side Club during the opening of the 2008 Venice Biennale. He calls parametricism the 'great new style after modernism' and suggests that, following a long wave of research and innovation, it has now 'achieved pervasive hegemony'.[7] The great virtue of parametric design is continuous differentiation within an otherwise uniform formal system, the results of which are systemic and unique, simple and complex, one and many.

The use of parametric tools and thinking appeared first in the work of architects such as Norman Foster. Initially it was a way of making complex two-dimensional surfaces for facades and roofs, such as the glass roof over the courtyard at the British Museum, and then it progressed into three-dimensional forms like the Gherkin in the City of London, where the structure remains relatively conventional and the complex form is achieved, once more, by shaping the glass envelope.

More recently, younger architects such as Ferda Kolatan and Erich Schoenenberger of su11 have explored the potential of parametric three-dimensional structures to merge the systematic and the plastic in a more synthetic way. Their Dune House for the desert of Nevada was commissioned by the Vitra Museum for Open House, an exhibition in 2007. Inspired by the root of a cactus, the designers used Bentley Systems's Generative Components software to extrapolate two-dimensional pattern into a three-dimensional, constructable and occupiable structure. Their digital model is sufficiently robust and malleable to incorporate all the formal inflections needed to accommodate the functions of domestic life (kitchens, bathrooms, closets, furnishings), to achieve environmental performance appropriate to the local ecology, and also to exist as a realisable structure.

Research like this might be seen to follow some of Santiago Calatrava's recent work with precast concrete, such as the Valencia Science Centre of 2000. However, this project does not incorporate the variation and customisation of components sought by Kolatan and Schoenenberger, for whom Pier Luigi Nervi's work in the 1940s and 1950s showed the way. Nervi's Exhibition Hall in Turin (1948–49) and the Palazzetto dello Sport in Rome (1958–59) used complex precast forms to create intricate patterns and structures of almost hypnotic beauty. His design for an unbuilt cathedral in New Norcia, Australia (1959–61) already demonstrated that the sizes and shapes of the units could be varied to create complex curvatures.

An even earlier example of this may be found,

surprisingly, in Bruno Taut's familiar Glass Pavilion of 1914. While known for its play with glass, the structure is, in fact, concrete, including a cupola of tiny reinforced-concrete ribs, which, as in the work of Nervi and su11, was inspired by natural models. With Taut's project, we come back to the topic of glass architecture; for Taut and Paul Scheerbart, this encompassed not only glass but other synthetic materials, including concrete and iron as well as a host of other new technologies. For Scheerbart, such advances promised to achieve a second nature with which to remake the crust of the Earth – one that neither opposes nor dominates nature but rather extends it, in the sense suggested by Schinkel. It was an optimistic vision of designers learning from nature in order to re-enchant a world that had been disenchanted by science and technology, not by rejecting modernity but by superseding the opposition of mechanical and organic in a new paradigm that would later be called biotechnic or bionic.

While parametric design may indeed yield a synthesis of the dialectic of rigour and expression, perhaps it would benefit from being released from that burden, freed of the dialectics of form, even residual ones, and resituated within a much larger, more diverse and polymorphous field of

architectural research and experimentation. If we follow Goethe's monistic parallels between human and other natures, might we not leave behind entirely the habit of mind that turns events into categories and pitches them against one another in such reductive ways? Perhaps it would be preferable to explore more freely the world depicted in 1838 by Joseph Michael Gandy in his image *Architecture: Its Natural Model*, updated to incorporate contemporary understandings of living processes and behaviour.

Joseph Michael Gandy,
Architecture: Its Natural Model,
1838

In that world, we might find that mutability is already pervasive. We might also find glorious puzzles, inspiring paradoxes and unfathomable totalities that caution against claims to definitive knowledge or formal systems, even parametric ones. We might even find that some of the most remarkable things in the world have already been produced through human ingenuity, including those made in concrete, whose plastic logic seems entirely at home here, producing unending variations, adaptations and transformations, and refusing to be pinned down.

NOTES

1. Sigfried Giedion, *Building in France. Building in Iron. Building in Ferro-Concrete*, trans. J. Duncan Berry (Santa Monica: Getty Center, 1995).

2. See Srdjan Jovanovic Weiss, 'Evasions of Temporality', in Ilka and Andreas Ruby, eds., *Urban Transformation* (Berlin: Ruby Press, 2008), 208–17.

3. Barry Bergdoll recently observed how widespread Goethe's influence was throughout the nineteenth and early twentieth centuries. See Bergdoll, 'Nature's Architecture: The Quest for the Laws of Form and the Critique of Historicism', in Angeli Sachs, ed., *Nature Design: From Inspiration to Innovation* (Baden/Zurich: Lars Müller Publishers and Museum für Gestaltung, 2007), 46–59.

4. Julius Vischer and Ludwig Hilberseimer, *Beton als Gestalter* (Stuttgart: J Hoffmann, 1928).

5. See Manfredo Tafuri, *Architecture and Utopia*, trans. Barbara Luigi La Penta (Cambridge, MA: MIT Press, 1976); and Manfredo Tafuri and Francesco Dal Co, *Modern Architecture*, trans. Robert Erich Wolf (New York: HN Abrams, 1979).

6. Jean-Louis Cohen, 'Modern Architecture and the Saga of Concrete', in Jean-Louis Cohen and G Martin Moeller Jr, eds., *Liquid Stone: New Architecture in Concrete* (New York: Princeton Architectural Press, 2006), 23–24.

7. Patrik Schumacher, 'Parametricism as Style – Parametricist Manifesto', delivered at the Dark Side Club, 11th Architecture Biennale, Venice 2008, published at www.patrikschumacher.com/Parametricism%20as%20Style.htm

IMAGE SECTION

GLASS ARCHITECTURE

Wenzel Hablik, Exhibition Tower, Variation 4A II, 1921
© Wenzel-Hablik-Foundation, Itzehoe

El Lissitzky, Der Wolkenbügel (Cloud Stirrup), 1924–25

ANYTHING BUT LITERAL

Bauhaus at Dessau, Walter Gropius and
Adolf Meyer Architects, 1925–26 © DACS

Rear elevation of the Villa Stein-de Monzie at Garches, Le Corbusier, 1927
© FLC / ADAGP and DACS

TRANSPARENCY:
AUTONOMY & RELATIONALITY

Charles-Edouard Jeanneret [Le Corbusier], Still Life for Pavillon
de l'Esprit Nouveau, 1924 © FLC / ADAGP and DACS

Le Corbusier, Quartiers modernes Frugès,
Bordeaux-Pessac, 1924–27 © FLC / ADAGP and DACS

UTOPIA OF GLASS

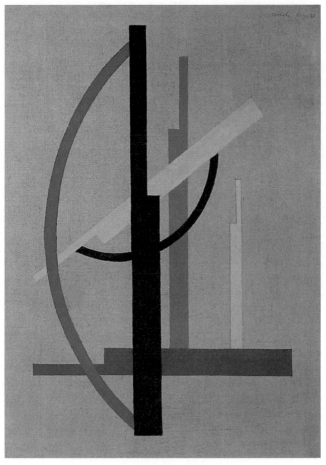

László Moholy-Nagy, *Glass Architecture* III, 1921–22
© Hattula Moholy-Nagy/DACS

Jan Kamman, 'Architecture', c. 1929
Courtesy of Rotterdam Municipal Collection

WALTER BENJAMIN AND THE
TECTONIC UNCONSCIOUS

Sigfried Giedion, Pont Transbordeur spanning the
industrial harbour of Marseilles gta Archives / ETH Zurich

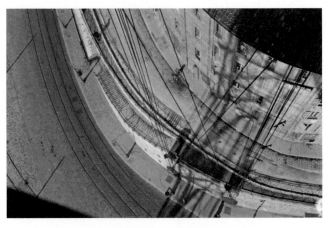

Sigfried Giedion, view from the Pont Transbordeur of a street alongside
the industrial harbour gta Archives / ETH Zurich

SAME DIFFERENCE

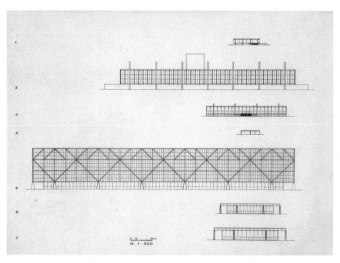

Office of Mies van der Rohe, elevations for seven clear-span buildings
drawn to uniform scale © DACS

Leaves from the field buttercup
(*Ranunculus acria*)

MIES'S EVENT SPACE

View of opening of the inaugural exhibition, Mondrian, at the
New National Gallery, Berlin, 1968 © DACS

Office of Mies van der Rohe, New National Gallery, Berlin, model
with hypothetical exhibition installation, 1964 © Chicago History Museum

BIOCONSTRUCTIVISMS

Two radiolarians, the *Reticulum plasmatique*, after Carnoy, and the *Aulonia hexagona*, as depicted by Ernst Haeckel. Courtesy of Dover

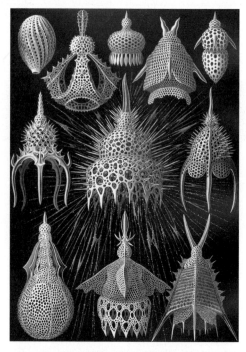

Ernst Haeckel, *Kunstformen der Natur* (1904)

PERVASIVE PLASTICITY

Joseph Michael Gandy, *Architecture: Its Natural Model*, 1838
Courtesy of the Trustees of Sir John Soane's Museum, London

Architecture Words 7
Modernity Unbound:
Other Histories of Architectural Modernity
Detlef Mertins

Series Editor: Brett Steele

AA Managing Editor: Thomas Weaver
AA Publications Editor: Pamela Johnston
AA Art Director: Zak Kyes
Design: Wayne Daly
Series Design: Wayne Daly, Zak Kyes
Editorial Assistant: Clare Barrett
Image research: Mollie Claypool

Set in P22 Underground Pro and Palatino

Printed in Belgium by Die Keure

ISBN 978-1-902902-89-0

Reprinted 2012

For a catalogue of AA Publications visit
aaschool.ac.uk/publications
or email publications@aaschool.ac.uk

AA Publications
36 Bedford Square
London WC1B 3ES
T +44 (0)20 7887 4021
F +44 (0)20 7414 0783